DEVELOPING
TOMORROW'S
LEADERS

The Association of Community College Trustees and Rowman & Littlefield Publishers

The Futures Series on Community Colleges

Sponsored by the Association of Community College Trustees and Rowman & Littlefield Publishers, *The Futures Series on Community Colleges* is designed to produce and deliver books that strike to the heart of issues that will shape the future of community colleges. *Futures* books examine emerging structures, systems, and business models, and stretch prevailing assumptions about leadership and management by reaching beyond the limits of convention and tradition.

Topics addressed in the *Series* are those that are vital to community colleges, but have yet to receive meaningful attention in literature, research, and analysis. *Futures* books are written by scholars and practitioners who deliver a unique perspective on a topic or issue—a president or higher education consultant bringing expert and practical understanding to a topic, a policy analyst breaking down a complex problem into component parts, an academic or think tank scholar conducting incisive research, or a researcher and a practitioner working together to examine an issue through different lenses.

Futures books are developed on the premise that disruptive innovation and industry transformation are, and will be, an ongoing challenge. Gradual improvement is, understandably, a natural preference of leaders. It will not be enough, however, to position our colleges for the future. The future will be about transformation and, to perform optimally, our colleges will need to become capable of large-scale change. As leaders come face-to-face with digital forces and rapidly changing social, economic, and public policy conditions, they will have no choice but to get ahead of change or relinquish market position to competitors. *Futures* books are a vehicle through which leaders can learn about and prepare for what's ahead. Whether it's through analysis of what big data will mean in the next generation of colleges, or which business models will become the new normal, *Futures* books are a resource for practitioners who realize that the ideas of out-of-the-box thinkers and the innovative practices of high-performing organizations can be invaluable for answering big questions and solving complex problems.

Richard L. Alfred, Series Co-Editor
Emeritus Professor of Higher Education
University of Michigan

Debbie Sydow, Series Co-editor
President
Richard Bland College of the College of
    William and Mary

Forthcoming Books in
The Futures Series on Community Colleges

Financing America's Community Colleges: Where We Are, Where We're Going
By Richard Romano and James Palmer
Grounded in an economic perspective, *Financing America's Community Colleges* helps college leaders make sense of the challenges they face in securing and managing the resources needed to carry out the community college mission. Finance has perpetually been an Achilles' heel for leaders at all levels of management. With the premise that leaders are better at winning battles they know something about, this book equips leaders with an understanding of the fundamentals and the complexities of community college finance. It tackles current and emerging issues with insight that is analytic and prophetic—a must-read for current and prospective leaders.

Unrelenting Change, Disruptive Innovation, and Risk: Forging the Next Generation of Community Colleges
By Daniel J. Phelan
In this book, thirty-five-year veteran Dan Phelan shares key insights from his personal and professional journey as a transformational, entrepreneurial community college leader. The book's wisdom and insights are amplified by observations gleaned from interviews and visits with dozens of leading practitioners. Drawing upon his sailing experiences, Phelan argues that leaders should stop playing it safe in the harbor because the real gains driving institutional and student success are found in uncharted waters. *Unrelenting Change, Disruptive Innovation, and Risk* dares community college leaders to innovate and provides them with a tool kit for understanding changing conditions, assessing risk, and successfully navigating change.

The Urgency of Now: Equity and Excellence
By Marcus M. Kolb, Samuel D. Cargile, et al.
The Urgency of Now asserts that in addition to being granted access to the community college, all twenty-first-century students need uncompromised support to succeed. Success means demonstrating relevant learning for transfer and employment and timely completion of credentials. Looking to the future, the authors contend that community colleges, both because of their past successes and future challenges, are at the epicenter for determining the essential ingredients of a new student-centered system that guarantees equity and excellence.

The Completion Agenda in Community Colleges: What It Is, Why It Matters, and Where It's Going
By Chris Baldwin
Community colleges in many states are facing intensifying pressure from policy makers for improved student outcomes overtly manifested in aggressive performance-based funding formulas. In this book, Chris Baldwin asks and answers an overarching question: Are community colleges, government agencies, foundations, and other entities aware of the unintended consequences of actions related to the completion agenda? The book explores the potential benefit of increased educational attainment and credentials versus the possible sacrifice of quality and the labor market value of the credentials awarded.

Institutional Analytics: Building a Culture of Evidence
By Karen Stout
Institutional Analytics paints a clear picture of the challenges involved in cultural change and building a team capable of using analytics to gain a competitive advantage for the future. Revealing that community colleges pretend to be more data driven than they actually are, Stout challenges leadership teams to set clear goals, define what success looks like, and ask the right questions to get there. By adopting new tools, abandoning legacy systems and relationships, and boldly adopting open source solutions, colleges can turn large quantities of data into business intelligence that drives transformation.

Previously Published Books in
The Series on Community Colleges

Minding the Dream: The Process and Practice of the American Community College, Second Edition
By Gail O. Mellow and Cynthia M. Heelan

First in the World: Community Colleges and America's Future
By J. Noah Brown

Community College Student Success: From Boardrooms to Classrooms
By Banessa Smith Morest

Re-visioning Community Colleges
By Debbie Sydow and Richard Alfred

Community Colleges on the Horizon: Challenge, Choice, or Abundance
By Richard Alfred, Christopher Shults, Ozan Jaquette, and Shelley Strickland

DEVELOPING TOMORROW'S LEADERS

Context, Challenges, and Capabilities

**Pamela L. Eddy,
Debbie L. Sydow,
Richard L. Alfred, and
Regina L. Garza Mitchell**

ASSOCIATION OF
COMMUNITY COLLEGE TRUSTEES

ROWMAN & LITTLEFIELD
Lanham • Boulder • New York • London

Published by Rowman & Littlefield
A wholly owned subsidiary of The Rowman & Littlefield Publishing Group,
Inc.
4501 Forbes Boulevard, Suite 200, Lanham, Maryland 20706
www.rowman.com

Unit A, Whitacre Mews, 26-34 Stannary Street, London SE11 4AB

British Library Cataloguing in Publication Information Available

Library of Congress Cataloging-in-Publication Data
Eddy, Pamela Lynn.
Developing tomorrow's leaders : context, challenges, and capabilities / Pamela
L. Eddy, Debbie L. Sydow, Richard L. Alfred, and Regina L. Garza Mitchell.
pages cm. — (The futures series on community colleges)
Includes index.
ISBN 978-1-4758-1100-1 (cloth : alk. paper) — ISBN 978-1-4758-2033-1
(pbk. : alk. paper) — ISBN 978-1-4758-1101-8 (electronic)
1. Community colleges—United States—Administration. 2. Community
college administrators—United States. 3. Educational leadership—United
States. I. Title.
LB2341.E334 2015
378.1''5430973—dc23
                                                                2015013035

∞™ The paper used in this publication meets the minimum requirements
of American National Standard for Information Sciences—Permanence of
Paper for Printed Library Materials, ANSI/NISO Z39.48-1992.

Printed in the United States of America

CONTENTS

FOREWORD

America's community colleges, like all of higher education, are at a significant crossroads. Technology, competition, reduced public resources, aging facilities, increased scrutiny, new mandates for accountability, aging leadership and faculty, a focus on student success and completion, and greater public reliance on the power of our colleges to transform lives and economies demand, as never before, a new type of leadership.

What has worked for our institutions in the past likely will not work in the future. Myriad challenges face our colleges, and an entirely different type of leadership is required if colleges are to navigate troubled waters. To meet these challenges, new thinking and new strategies for developing leaders are required.

As the president and chief executive officer of the Association of Community College Trustees (ACCT), which is an organization that is deeply invested in developing leaders that are capable of meeting these challenges, I wholeheartedly embrace the opportunity to copublish the Futures Series on Community Colleges books with Rowman & Littlefield. And I could not be happier that the first title in this series is a powerful and necessary contribution to the needed revolution in preparing today's and tomorrow's community college leaders.

The authors, Pamela Eddy, Debbie Sydow, Dick Alfred, and Regina Garza Mitchell, deliver a portent of the future and a road map for how we can, and *must*, shift the developmental path for leaders to bring community colleges successfully into their second century. With deep experience in community college leadership and research and policy realms, the authors describe current leader development shortcomings, leavening their critique with clarity of vision, focused recommendations, and strategies for improvement. As they point out, "*Who* leads our colleges and *how* they lead makes the difference between success and failure."

To make the case for new leadership, the authors use three tableaus describing leadership of the past, the present, and, most important, the future. Referring to the leadership pipeline of the past as linear, the book correctly identifies innovation as the marker for the future. Because today's leaders are constrained by the pressing nature of immediate challenges, future success will be realized through the strategic capability of leaders to articulate a new game plan internally and externally that will power wholesale reinvention from the inside out.

Today's leaders are focused almost entirely on resources and competitive positioning. All of higher education seems intent on becoming bigger, more comprehensive, and defined by ancillary services and benefits for students. Increasing competition from the for-profit sector, and among and between community colleges themselves, consumes the attention of leaders and governing boards. The complexity of circumstances taxes presidents' abilities, resulting all too often in reliance on old solutions that are ill-suited to meet current and future challenges.

A new style of leadership is needed that leverages the virtually unlimited power of internal and external networks if our colleges are to focus on their core mission and ensure their competitive position in the higher education market. In short, the authors argue that leadership capability must be strategically developed and deployed to enable transformation, and "transformation is an imperative for *every* college."

Turning to leaders of the future, the book forcefully argues for new approaches and a decided break from how we traditionally have prepared and advanced leaders through our institutions. To meet the growing demand for new leaders and to confront the tsunami of retirements and shortened tenure of presidents, the authors correctly suggest that we abandon our traditional assumptions and expectations regarding how our leaders "should" look and act. Forces that are redefining society and how we interact, learn, and acquire information must be embraced by leaders and incorporated into strategies for transformation.

Current leadership development models embedded in graduate programs, leadership academies, fellowships, and the like, must be rethought. The skills that our leaders need now and in the future cannot be honed through curricula that focus on past models or theories. Studying entrepreneurial and leading business practices and focusing on innovation, analytics, and "big data" lend themselves more readily to cultivating and embedding the strategic and visioning skills necessary to enable our institutions to improve their performance and maintain competitive advantage.

The final chapter of the book, "Strategically Looking Forward," creates the road map that we will need to follow. "Networked Leadership" must become the hallmark for the future. And a growing familiarity with information and analytics, a total rethinking of resources, and an ability to leverage new partnerships must become the fuel that leaders use to drive innovation. Leaders must evolve into cocreators and design experts, imbued with discrete values and a vision for the future. This is the new leadership imperative. Status quo is not an option. As the authors so appropriately suggest in the final words of the book, "our colleges and their students expect and should receive nothing less."

J. Noah Brown
President and CEO
Association of Community College Trustees
Washington, D.C.

ACKNOWLEDGMENTS

It takes time, patience, and a great deal of support to write a book. We gratefully acknowledge the people who helped us achieve our goal. First, we are thankful for the leaders with whom we have served and who provided inspiration for many of the ideas in this book. We are especially grateful to those leaders who took the time to share their thoughts on leadership development and the future of leadership. Although we were not able to include all of their words and ideas in the book, we learned from each of them: James Lorenson, Regina Peruggi, Gerardo de los Santos, Carol Lucey, Mark Milliron, Diane Troyer, Deanna Sheppard, Deborah Shephard, Daniel Larson, Feliccia Moore-Davis, Larry Ebbers, James Sawyer, Al Lorengo, and Lori Gaskin.

Second, we spent a significant amount of time together as coauthors developing and sharing ideas, advancing different points of view, and shaping the message we wanted to deliver to leaders. Writing this book became a unique learning opportunity in its own right—a seminar involving colleagues brought together by a passion for leadership, a belief that we can do better, and a take-no-prisoners attitude. We were able to push our thinking forward in ways not possible if this had been a solo venture.

Finally, appreciation is extended to current and future leader generations serving in our nation's community colleges. It is through the unflagging efforts of so many on the ground that student lives are changed.

As analysts of community college leadership, it is often easy to pontificate about what leaders should think and do, how they should behave, and what they should embrace and adopt. Yet, it is the reality check of talking with sitting leaders that provides the true test. We are privileged to have spent time on many community college campuses testing ideas, challenging assumptions, and witnessing what happens when transformative change occurs. To be sure, change is a messy process, but it is reality for our colleges and it is not going to go away.

A special thanks goes to Tehmina Khwaja, PhD, at the College of William and Mary for her assistance in final formatting of this work. Her attention to detail and questioning helped provide polish to the chapters. As Series Editors, Richard Alfred and Debbie Sydow provided unfailing leadership and support for this effort. The opportunity to coauthor with them was truly a gift.

Pamela Eddy: The never-ending support of my husband, David Pape, provided the time and space needed to complete this book. Regina Garza Mitchell continues to be a critical member of my community of practice. Dick Alfred, a fellow alumnus of Allegheny College, expanded my thinking in ways for which I'm forever grateful. Debbie Sydow exemplified what it means to be a transformational leader.

Debbie Sydow: Engaging in a yearlong conversation about the future of community college leadership with intellectual heavyweights like Dick Alfred, Pam Eddy, and Regina Garza Mitchell was an extraordinary professional development opportunity. It turns out that when theorists and practitioners come together as prognosticators, strange and wondrous things happen. Special appreciation goes to Vernon R. Lindquist for reading early drafts and offering insightful and incisive feedback that proved useful for chiseling.

Dick Alfred: The opportunity to write a book on leadership in the twilight of a forty-five-year career dedicated to community colleges as a research university academic and senior administrator in three community college districts has been a privilege. Working with three colleagues in an ongoing no-holds-barred seminar became a shaping experience for all of us as well as a medium for generating new ideas on leadership. It is my wish that the ideas advanced in this book will drive colleges, and those who lead them, to new heights of performance in a ride to the future that will be charged with risk, challenge, and opportunity.

Regina Garza Mitchell: Many thanks to my friend and mentor, Pamela Eddy, for inviting me to be a part of this experience and for her unflagging energy throughout the process. Dick Alfred and Debbie Sydow pushed me to think differently and to question my thoughts on and approaches to leadership. I've learned from each of you and am grateful for the opportunity to work with such great thinkers. As always, I am most grateful for Joseph Mitchell and his unfailing confidence in my ability to get things done and for providing the love and encouragement to do so.

1

SETTING THE CONTEXT

> In recent years, technology and globalization have changed our way
> of life more than anyone could have imagined. While enriching us
> in many ways, these forces also have eliminated traditionally secure
> jobs and eroded economic security for millions. Now, we face an
> urgent national challenge: finding new strategies that help all Ameri-
> cans flourish in today's economy.[1]
>
> —Markle Economic Future Initiative

The higher education industry is in the midst of a revolution, as are so
many other industries that thrived during the industrial era and have
been slow to respond to the new mandates for success in the information age. Although many of the ideas and principles presented in this
book are applicable to other institutions of higher education and perhaps to other industries, our focus is on community colleges and their
leadership challenges and opportunities during this period of transformation brought on by the digital revolution.

Community colleges, once relegated to the backwaters of postsecondary education, are now firmly established in the mainstream of American higher education. Despite unparalleled growth and critical acclaim,
community colleges find themselves at a crossroads. Erosion of public
funding, a sustained push for college completion, increased scrutiny of

student outcomes, and a host of other challenges threaten their viability and contribute to a landscape that is anything but stable. *Who* leads our colleges and *how* they lead makes a difference between success and failure.

In the brief history of community colleges, never has the need for purposeful attention to developing leaders been more important. The reasons—changing rules of competition, executive retirements, forced separations, cultural intransigence, and diminishing interest in mobility among second-tier administrators—are some of the factors impacting leader supply and demand.[2] Combined with environmental turbulence and rapid-scale change, these factors make leader preparation among the most pervasive of issues facing community colleges.

Many of the presidents during the founding era of community colleges enjoyed long tenure and eased into retirement before the onset of reduction.[3] Coupled with a changing of the guard of seasoned leaders was mission sprawl[4] and concomitant changes in programming, organizational architecture, and governance.

Growth born of accretion had the advantage of enhancing legitimacy in the eyes of the public, but the disadvantage of stretching capacity to a breaking point as public support failed to keep pace with enrollment.[5] Multiple and competing demands on resources have enmeshed community colleges in a conundrum that defies easy resolution. They are at the center of a tension between two worlds—one in which they are praised as purveyors of opportunity and the other in which they are criticized as impediments to student achievement.

LEADING COMMUNITY COLLEGES

Entering this environment are prospective and aspiring leaders who are not adequately prepared for the complexities of managing in a paradoxical organization. Inside the organization are long-serving instructors and staff who lament the loss of a cherished past and ask: *Who would want to lead in this landscape?*[6]

Outside the organization are constituencies who expect leaders to turn the organization on a dime. Leadership has become a rocky ride with rewards counterbalanced by risk—a context dramatically different from the formative period when colleges operated in a stable environment. The context continues to evolve and—to the chagrin of many—at a pace that challenges the capacity of leaders.

To illustrate the extent and direction of change, we have created three tableaus—one of leadership practice in the past, one illustrating the challenges leaders face today, and one looking forward into the future. Although these tableaus provide only a limited view of the work of leaders, they illustrate the depth and intensity of change in conditions and circumstances that form the context for leadership. This contrast sets the stage for understanding the relationship between context and leadership that is central to this book.

Leading Yesterday

Leaders of first-generation community colleges worked in an environment dramatically different from today in terms of the scope, scale, and complexity of operations. There were needs and challenges to address, indeed, as there always are with start-up organizations.

Community colleges, however, were different; they had clarity with regard to the bottom line. They were in the business of opportunity and growth, making the work of leaders purposeful in nature. Funding streams, although compromised by finance formulas favoring four-year colleges and universities, were predictable, and resource flows were steady.

The mission was clear, and colleges were led by presidents deeply committed to the philosophy and purpose of a distinctly different type of institution where access was of paramount importance and enrolling as many students as possible, many of whom were first-generation, was foremost in the minds of leaders.

Decision making in early-generation colleges could be best described as top-down with most variables known or anticipated. Cost-benefit tallies and easily observed results were the best test of a decision outcome.[7] For colleges working with constrained resources, making something out of nothing was often the true test of institutional and leadership effectiveness. Leaders and staff worked with limited information as external scanning, technology-supported data platforms, effectiveness models, and analytics were decades away. Strategic planning was just coming into focus,[8] and projections were built on a linear platform. The scope of information required to make decisions was manageable, and results were generally predictable. Once a community college was established, leading typically involved incremental change in contrast to wholesale transformation.

Leader mobility in yesterday's colleges can best be described as linear: an individual started as an instructor and moved first to department chair, then to dean or provost, and eventually to president.[9] As a result, presidents were well aware of the work of personnel in a wide range of positions and understood the basics of what was required to operate a college. True, there was a learning curve when entering the executive office, but this had more to do with role transition than lack of awareness about the nature and scope of the position.

Management was top-down in small-scale colleges with a simple organizational chart and a large proportion of full-time instructors. Communication was relatively straightforward as information flowed easily among a small core of staff, and the time required to transmit important pieces of information was short.

A permanent core of full-time instructors provided a face for the college in the community and took care of the business of academe.[10] Instructors worked with multiple portfolios, developing courses and curricula, teaching and advising students, hashing out articulation agreements with regional colleges, and building partnerships with community organizations.

The task of teaching diverse students in an open-door institution made the role of instructor both challenging and absorbing. There was no subtlety or mystery about what was expected of them. Their job was to teach and to open the door to opportunity through classroom instruction that prepared learners for work and further education.

The challenge of leading in early-generation colleges was also relatively straightforward. Students came directly from high school with different levels of preparation, the majority requiring remediation. The convenience of open admissions, low cost, and proximity attracted large numbers of adults, particularly women with families, creating a mix of students unduplicated by traditional colleges and universities.[11]

Leaders were managing institutions that were smaller; these colleges faced fewer challenges, in general, and they were predictably resourced in terms of operating and capital expenditures. These leaders were conversant with forces in the environment, knew more about instructors and staff on their campuses, and faced fewer demands from external publics. Leadership was not without its challenges, of course, but there was a predictable form and flow to the work of a president. CEOs understood what they would face on the job when assuming the position: becoming familiar with the campus and community, managing the board, and extending the reach of the college.[12] In retrospect, yesterday's presidents were working in an era of stability in which problems were predictable and solvable, and the resources they had to work with were known.

Leading Today

The dynamic nature of today's world has created what some have labeled the *new normal*. Change is rapid and broad in scale, and leaders must be creative to overcome challenges that were either unseen or not present in the past. Institutions and leaders are working in a landscape that can best be described as contradictory.

Community colleges have grown and matured into comprehensive organizations with established patterns of funding, operation, and education delivery. This sector has gained recognition as a key player in the nation's P–20 education system. Never before have they been in the national spotlight like community colleges are today as states and localities ramp up to prepare workers for digital-age jobs and families seek affordable alternative to pricey college degrees. Who could have imaged even a decade ago that the president of the United States would put forth a proposal to make a community college education free to all Americans as he did in 2015?

With this newfound understanding and appreciation of the community college sector, expectations are greater, resources are increasingly austere, and the future is wildly uncertain. Community colleges have been perpetually underfunded and have compensated by perfecting the art of stretching limited public funds.[13] Cited by many as a model of how to achieve more with less, leaders have learned—many the hard way—that accolades are not a substitute for resources.

In a postrecessionary economy, public funding does not readily rebound to previous levels. Growth is achieved through collaboration, creative programming, and networks created to tap a wide range of resources. Networks, however, are a different breed and pose a new set of challenges to institutions and leaders. To be effective, they require flexible structures and systems and an organizational mind-set that embraces risk and change, which is a departure for leaders and staff accustomed to the status quo and a slower pace of change.

Further complicating the landscape are changing rules of competition. Community colleges now face competition from each other, from public and private four-year colleges, and from for-profit providers. Proprietary institutions equipped with aggressive sales tactics and sophisticated online delivery platforms have entered an arena that historically was the domain of community colleges. These institutions offer the advantage of increased flexibility for admission and program completion. So, too, do universities through the medium of entrepreneurial units, schools of continuing studies, and a variety of online education resources.

Students with a growing array of options expect more and better service. They demand access to education when they want it, how they want it, and where they want it. An emphasis on just-in-time and competency-based learning has leveled the playing field, and community colleges no longer hold the advantage. As a sitting president noted, "The operational model that got us to this point is insufficient to get us to the future."[14]

In addition, the student body in early-generation colleges was considerably less diverse. Traditional-aged and high school students make up more of the student body today. Students are not only more ethnically diverse; they manifest wider gaps in academic preparation, and a high school credential can take many different forms.

Colleges have responded by adjusting programs and services to reach students with changing needs and preferences. Among them are honors programs, dual enrollment, and sundry initiatives with P–12 schools that are designed to improve student preparation for college. There are also early college high school and various forms of retooled developmental courses and curricula to address perhaps the most pernicious deterrent to degree completion—academic underpreparedness.

Course-taking patterns are shifting, with more students taking courses at multiple institutions, often concurrently, as "swirlers."[15] These new cohorts of students are placing dramatically different demands on systems that are, by and large, ill-prepared to respond to millennials and the i-generation.

Community college instructors and staff are collaborating with P–12 teachers and administrators to intervene earlier in the education pipeline to prepare students for the rigors of college attendance and to improve their readiness for success. Support programs such as supplemental instruction and access to college coaches are being offered in high schools to help ease the transition.

Similarly, community colleges are reaching upward to ease the transfer process for students moving on to four-year colleges and universities. In some states, colleges are offering baccalaureate degrees, or they are hosting higher education centers that provide on-campus baccalaureate- and graduate-level courses delivered by college and university partners. These courses and programs, delivered predominantly by part-time faculty, are being offered in face-to-face, online, and hybrid formats.

The environment for faculty differs considerably from a previous and simpler time when full-time instructors delivered the bulk of instruction with a piece of chalk in hand and students sitting before them in neat rows of desks. Today's instructors are expected to deliver teaching content in a variety of formats and modalities, to diversify their teaching strategies to meet a wide range of learning preferences and abilities, and to infuse technology into classroom teaching.[16]

These expectations can be overwhelming for faculty members who are teaching heavy course loads and receiving little in the way of professional development. Such expectations can be even more detrimental to part-time faculty who typically receive minimal compensation, lack support from full-time colleagues, and feel distanced from the organization.

Leaders, too, are finding themselves in foreign territory where the surroundings, language, and the tools are mysterious and strange. The complexity of the environment requires them to employ a style that is more collaborative and creative than they might have considered in the past. Partnerships with other colleges, business and industry, P–12 schools, and community organizations are now commonplace.

Decision-making models of the past that delivered information through a chain of command are increasingly ineffective. Now leaders must factor chaos into the decision process and use data to inform planning and enhance organizational learning.[17] As more and more colleges embrace analytics, the use of data to inform decision making has become central to operations. Figuring out how to improve practice, how to question assumptions, and how to involve a wide array of stakeholders in governance is essential for today's leaders.

In the words of Dan Phelan, president of Jackson College, "This, I believe, is the community college's best time in terms of defining the moment and deciding what we will become for the future—what this country needs us to be and what states and localities need us to be. This is not for the faint of heart."[18]

Given the turbulent environment in which today's colleges operate, pipelines and career pathways for leaders are opening up in ways never before possible. Alternative pathways enable individuals with different background experience and skill sets to enter positions of leadership. For example, more presidents are entering leadership positions from outside community colleges.[19] They are coming from business and health organizations, four-year colleges, government agencies, and the military. They are more diverse in race, gender, ethnicity, and background. These new leaders bring a different perspective, and they are not shy about questioning old ways of operating—systems, decision-making processes, and culture.

Leaders in today's colleges generally subscribe to innovation and exhibit a passion for student success, which is the new mandate and mission. They understand the important role that community colleges play in contributing to the economic vitality of communities. Creativity, risk tolerance, and strategic thinking are valued leadership attributes. Today's successful leaders have learned that a college is not unlike a business, and there are certain resources required for success: technology to build responsive systems, data to inform decisions and measure success, and revenue from nontraditional sources to support operations.

Leaders in today's community colleges work in a high-stakes environment that demands not only solid resource management to drive strategic goals, but also robust relationships with multiple external constituencies. These leaders have many masters, from boards to legislators to accrediting bodies to business partners to students to faculty. It is a deep and wide network of stakeholders, all of whom hold leaders accountable for higher and higher levels of institutional performance. Those who approach leadership with a business-as-usual mentality are likely to fail, but those who embrace the realities of the new norm and carefully prepare to lead in this dynamic environment will surely thrive.

Leading Tomorrow

Turbulence, change, transformation—these are watchwords for tomorrow's leaders. Predicting the future is difficult, but in turbulent times it is almost impossible. Rapidly changing conditions turn prediction into extrapolation of what is already known. Leaders seeking to minimize risk are understandably reluctant to make decisions based on speculation. What is known, therefore, becomes what is safe, and herein is a paradox. In the words of Einstein, "We cannot solve problems with the same thinking we used when we created them."

Leaders seeking foresight into the future will have no choice but to move beyond the known—to think outside the box, to break frames, and to think strategically. They will need to anticipate and read changing environmental forces, monitor organizations and industries, and pursue opportunities for innovation. Risk tolerance will become a new core competency for community college leaders.

Think back for a moment to a community college leader planning for the future in the 1970s. Two overriding forces—continuing expansion of market demand for postsecondary education and a commitment to open access—would lead to one planning conclusion: continued linear growth. Obviously, a singular focus on growth would miss evolving forces of resource decline, advancing technology, and shifting demographics. Perpetual growth as an ideology and a mandate for community colleges was adopted on the basis of conditions that brought early success to these institutions, but this ideology laid the groundwork for later failure.[20]

Foresight into the future requires speculation about what could be and a willingness to embrace risk and the possibility of failure. What follows is a snapshot of forces and conditions that could prevail in a landscape that will be anything but stable as higher education reinvents itself to align with the needs and demands of the twenty-first century.

Forces, Conditions, and Trends

Innovation will be the name of the game for community colleges. Changing constituencies with rapidly changing needs and expectations will be ubiquitous. Colleges will be forced to innovate to get in front and to stay in front of change. As conditions become more volatile, community colleges will have no choice but to create and deliver services in new and distinctively different ways and, by doing so, unknowingly open the door to disruptive innovation.

Challenges will come quickly and without warning in the form of rapidly changing external forces that disrupt operations by consuming fixed resources, competitive pressure from rivals delivering superior products and services at a low profit margin, and escalating expectations for performance by external stakeholders. The market conditions described illustrate the landscape that institutions and leaders will encounter:

- *Environmental forces will strengthen in intensity and impact.* Goods and services readily available in the past will become increasingly scarce and drive up costs as institutions compete for them; fixed costs will consume a larger share of institutional operating budgets and limit resources available for innovation.
- *Education-to-work linkages will be strengthened.* Global competition will increase the urgency for preparation and credentialing of workers with world-class skills in an increasingly digital world. Tightly structured school-to-college-to-business linkages will be created to reduce leaky pipelines from education to work.
- *Rules of competition will change.* Advancing technology will reduce the cost of market entry and enable new competitors to enter the postsecondary education market. Community colleges will experience budgetary strain as resources are expended to maintain market share to offset gains made by rivals through serial innovation in service delivery, programming, and systems and processes.
- *Community colleges will lose distinctiveness as a sector through merger and acquisition.* Some colleges will be integrated with baccalaureate institutions as part of a holistic service model, whereas others will be segmented into different service markets on the basis of unique organizational characteristics (location, students served, program-service mix, degrees awarded, funding streams, etc.).
- *Boundaries between college and community will become more permeable.* Resources and information will be widely shared among organizations as data systems are connected across community colleges, P–12, universities, state agencies, and private vendors.

Collective problem solving involving multiple partners will become standard operating practice.

- *Big data and analytics will reshape teaching, learning, and operational practice.* Business trends such as cloud-based services, predictive analytics, big data, social media analytics, and mobile computing will merge with higher education delivery systems (online education resources, competency-based credit, and student learning outcomes measures) to change the student learning experience and how institutions work.
- *Networks will evolve as a business model.* Networks will become a preferred model for organizational development because of the efficiency they bring to institutions (e.g., cost reduction and resource optimization); the structure of the network will ultimately become more important than the structure of the college in optimizing performance.
- *New models of accountability and accreditation will emerge.* Educational attainment will be tracked and analyzed across the P–20 continuum against standards created by public and private investors.
- *Private support will supplant traditional revenue streams as the basis for institutional operations.* Continuing declines in public support will force colleges to turn to private vendors and donors for support; a larger voice in resource allocation and operations will be the price of private support.
- *Externally driven conceptions of performance will supplant institutional conceptions in the definition of institutional success.* External constituencies will become a driving force in program design and student learning outcomes to ensure that college performance meets real-world expectations.

Institutional Implications

Colleges of the future will be closely connected with sending and receiving organizations, tightly connected with employers, P–12 schools, and community organizations. They will also be globally connected. These connections will provide for an exchange of best practices with organizations working together and learning from one another. The demands of business and society will require high levels of interpersonal and global competency. Students will need to possess not only soft skills, but also be comfortable with cultural diversity, foreign customs, and interactions with others around the world. Part and parcel of intercultural competence will be the ability to speak different languages.

Two factors will be of central importance in this expanded worldview of community college operations. First, instructors will become leaders in bringing community colleges into a globally connected and competitive world. Second, the perspectives of a wider group of stakeholders will be sought in program design and delivery.

No longer will instructors be principally responsible for curriculum design, teaching, and learning outcomes. There will be a backward-design approach to achieving the end goal—student success—that dictates who is involved at what stages of the education process. Reconstituted as a flexible and distributed professional workforce, faculty with responsibility for documented student learning outcomes and optimal career preparation will directly engage in industry dialogue with business and community partners and continuously infuse what is learned into courses and curricula.

In addition, faculty might very well play an expanded role in governance as their contribution to governance is likely to change as a new generation of leaders more effectively uses talent throughout the organization.[21]

Leaders will grow alternative revenue streams, institute operational efficiencies, and broker collaboration with a wide range of partners. They will move beyond a view of campus operations as a zero-sum game. Complex problems will be solved collectively through the expertise and efforts of multiple partners and stakeholders. College leaders will rely more on adaptive change[22] to address problems with no known solutions.

Leaders will also see the world differently. Failures will occur, but savvy leaders will see them not as a blow to their ego or career, but as a learning opportunity. New leadership skills aptly described by Johansen[23] will emerge in the future—"maker" instinct, clarity, dilemma flipping, immersive learning ability, bio-empathy, constructive depolarization, quiet transparency, smart mob organizing, and commons creating.

Notable in these traits is a focus on continuous learning, collaboration, and communication. Leaders in the future will be adept at crafting a cultural narrative of the college and creating a compelling vision of the future.

DEVELOPING TOMORROW'S LEADERS

These leadership tableaus place in stark relief the changing context in which community college leaders work. Colleges are moving quickly to alter their business model in response to changing conditions, but not quickly enough to keep up with the pace of change. Environmental forces will push them to think in new and different ways about leadership—who these leaders will be and the skills they will need to succeed.

These environmental forces alone will not, however, impel leaders and boards to prioritize the identification and development of leaders for tomorrow. Leaders today face severe and immediate challenges and have little choice but to focus on the present. These leaders are uncomfortable with the cries for new business models and innovation, and they question the need to change. Their reluctance to embrace change is understandable given the scary conditions they are facing. It leaves unanswered, however, the larger question of how to identify and develop leaders capable of solving the challenges that tomorrow's colleges will face.

Community college leaders emerge from a variety of starting points. Regardless of their trajectory, however, the primary source for development and training has been formally organized leadership programs sponsored by national associations, foundations, and research universities. Herein is a root cause of what we believe to be a deficit in the development of leaders with strategic skills.

These programs are designed to serve individuals identified as aspiring to leadership in contrast to those with latent or unexpressed interest. Most, if not all, of these programs focus on the acquisition of operational skills, such as budgeting and curriculum development, which, although an important knowledge base for leaders, do not prepare individuals for the larger demands of visioning and leveraging change in a complex organization.

Existing programs also neglect the development of faculty leaders, an area of increased importance in leveraging institutional resources to drive outcomes. Clearly what we are currently doing in the way of leader preparation is not enough. New strategies for leader development are needed to prepare the strategically focused, risk-embracing leaders our colleges will need in the future.

This book fills this gap by focusing on the strategic basis for community college leadership development and the skill sets that current and aspiring leaders will need to bring to these complex, fast-evolving institutions. The chapters that follow explain why contemporary leaders and governing boards need to reenvision and rethink community college leadership and the programs designed to identify and grow these leaders. Examples from the field are liberally used to provide insight into what creative leaders of the future should know and be able to do.

NOTES

1. The Markle Economic Future Initiative, *Rework America,* 2012, 3, http://www.reworkamerica.org/files/ReworkAmericaOverviewZ.pdf.

2. Pamela L. Eddy, *Community College Leadership: A Multidimensional Model for Leading Change* (Sterling, VA: Stylus Press, 2010).

3. Iris M. Weisman and George B. Vaughan, *The Community College Presidency: 2006* (Washington, DC: American Association of Community Colleges, 2007), http://www.aacc.nche.edu/Publications/Briefs/Pages/rb091420071.aspx.

4. Barbara K. Townsend and Kevin J. Dougherty, eds., *Community College Missions in the 21st Century. New Directions for Community Colleges*, no. 136. (San Francisco: Jossey-Bass, 2007).

5. Richard M. Romano, "Looking Behind Community College Budgets for Future Policy Considerations," *Community College Review* 40 (2012): 165–189, doi:10.1177/0091552112441824.

6. Kate Moser, "California's Community Colleges Struggle to Recruit and Retain Presidents," *Chronicle of Higher Education,* November 21, 2008, http://chronicle.com/article/California-s-Community/7524.

7. Ellen E. Chaffee, *Rational Decision Making in Higher Education: An NCHEMS Executive Overview* (Boulder: National Center for Higher Education Management Systems, 1983).

8. George Keller, *Academic Strategy: The Management Revolution in American Higher Education* (Baltimore: The Johns Hopkins University Press, 1983).

9. Marilyn J. Amey, Kim E. VanDerLinden, and Dennis F. Brown, "Career Mobility and Administrative Issues: A Twenty Year Comparison of the Changing Face of Community Colleges," *Community College Journal of Research and Practice* 26, no. 7–8 (2002): 573–589.

10. Brent D. Cejda and John B. Murray, eds., *Hiring the Next Generation of Faculty. New Directions for Community Colleges*, No. 152 (San Francisco: Jossey-Bass, 2010).

11. Virginia Montero-Hernandez and Christine Cerven, "Adult Student Development: The Agentic Approach to and its Relationship to the Community College Context," in *Understanding Community Colleges*, eds. John. S. Levin and Susan. T. Kater (New York: Routledge, 2013), 69–86.

12. Marilyn J. Amey, "Leadership: Community College Transitions," in *Understanding Community Colleges*, eds. John. S. Levin and Susan. T. Kater (New York: Routledge, 2013), 135–152.

13. Jim Palmer, "State Fiscal Support for Community Colleges," in *Understanding Community Colleges*, eds. John. S. Levin and Susan. T. Kater (New York: Routledge, 2013), 171–184.

14. Personal communication, Dan Phelan, president of Jackson College, Jackson, MI, e-mail message to author, February 18, 2014.

15. Victor M. H. Borden, (2004). "Accommodating Student Swirl," *Change* 36 no. 2 (2004): 10–17.

16. Mary Deane Sorcinelli, Ann E. Austin, Pamela L. Eddy, and Andrea L. Beach, *Creating the Future of Faculty Development: Learning from the Past, Understanding the Present* (Bolton, MA: Anker Publishing, 2006).

17. Adrianna Kezar, *How Colleges Change: Understanding, Leading, and Enacting Change* (New York: Routledge, 2013).

18. Personal communication, Dan Phelan, president of Jackson College, Jackson, MI, interview, October 14, 2013.

19. *The American College President 2012* (Washington, DC: American Council on Education, 2012).

20. Richard Alfred, "Leaders, Leveraging, and Abundance: Competencies for the Future," in *Leading for the Future: Alignment of the AACC Competencies with Practice. New Directions for Community Colleges*, 159, ed. Pamela L. Eddy (San Francisco: Jossey-Bass, 2012), 109–120.

21. Cathy N. Davidson, "Down With 'Service,' Up With Leadership," *Chronicle of Higher Education*, November 11, 2013, http://chronicle.com/article/Down-With-Service-Up-With/142897/.

22. Ronald, A. Heifetz, *Leadership without Easy Answers* (Cambridge: Harvard University Press, 1994).

23. Bob Johansen, *Leaders Make the Future: Ten New Leadership Skills for an Uncertain Future* (San Francisco: Berrett-Koehler, 2010).

2

CHANGE AND ORGANIZATIONAL TRANSFORMATION

"Is College a Lousy Investment?" . . . . That is the tone of the national conversation right now. It's not just experts, lawmakers, and disgruntled academics who see problems in the industry. Now parents, students, employers, and pundits say higher education is fundamentally broken—inefficient, ineffective, overpriced, outdated, out of touch.

—David Schwen[1]

When John Sperling established the University of Phoenix in the 1970s as a strikingly new and different alternative to traditional colleges, his intent was not to create a Fortune 500 company, but rather to provide working adults access to education and credentials that had previously been unavailable. Sperling tapped a demographic that traditional colleges missed; he implemented a new business model, and he adopted new technologies to deliver academic products and services to this previously untapped market. In so doing, Sperling commoditized education in a way that would set off a chain reaction and shake up the world of higher education for decades to come.

Fast-forward to 2010. With student loan debt spiraling and old ivory tower notions about the sanctity of the academy crumbling in the popular media and in popular opinion, Peter Thiel demonstrated his

utter lack of confidence in American colleges and universities by pay-
ing promising young entrepreneurs $100,000 to drop out of college and
instead pursue their start-up dreams, which planted one more seed of
doubt in a system that was once considered to be the surest route to
economic success and a good life.[2] The widespread attention that Thiel's
experiment continues to receive reflects a growing uncertainty among
employers and students about the value of a college degree and, more
broadly, about the future of higher education. Where do community
colleges fit in this massive industry transformation that is currently underway, and what are the implications for leaders?

Let us begin with the obvious. Leading a college today is fundamentally different than it was twenty years ago. Leaders are witnessing firsthand what *The Economist* described as "disruptive waves . . .
threatening to upend established ways of teaching and learning."[3] They
are hobbled by reduced funding stemming from sustained government
disinvestment in higher education and tuition that cannot keep pace
with cost.

Critics point to questionable leadership and argue that the resource
challenge facing higher education is, in part, caused by management
practices that have squandered resources and marginalized quality.[4]
Often mentioned is the growing reliance on part-time instructors, sub-
standard assessment practices, failure to eliminate obsolete programs,
marginal student outcomes, and technology investment running behind
competitors in a high-speed market.[5]

Leaders, in turn, argue that forces of change are largely beyond their
control and that prudence dictates caution. Regardless of the view
taken, waves of disruption and austere resources constitute a one-two
punch that has left leaders struggling to achieve equilibrium.

What is equilibrium? For many, it is the core delivery of programs
and services with an adequate budget invested in faculty and staff who
envision a future that looks much like the past. At the heart of this
model are employees holding positions that have remained fundamentally unchanged for decades. The status quo remains stubborn in the
face of change.

The organizations and their employees have withstood funding short-
falls, accountability mandates, and a drive for efficiency that has resulted
in an unbalanced workforce that is heavily reliant on part-timers. One

would think that this growing dependence on a part-time workforce would change the organizational structures and rules of the game. Part-time employees need resources and continuous support to ensure quality, and by virtue of sheer numbers, they are a management challenge.[6]

Remarkably, however, the structures and rules have held fast, and part-time hiring continues unabated. It is the fuel that keeps the growth engine running.[7] What colleges are left with is an operating model resembling a jigsaw puzzle with ill-fitting pieces. Educational content is tethered to traditional curricula and programming, and it is delivered through this cadre of part-time faculty, along with the largely autonomous tenured faculty who typically have little incentive to innovate. Clearly this is not the best foundation on which to build an institution that is capable of delivering superior student learning outcomes.

Community college leaders will need to be nimble to address the challenges facing their institutions. Not only are they facing a quantum shift in the landscape in which colleges are operating, but also a scope and speed of change unlike any they have ever experienced. One need only look to the enrollment contraction in 2012 and 2013 to understand the effect of a sudden change in operating conditions.[8]

Following unprecedented growth between 2008 and 2011, colleges set their sights on expansion that did not happen. The 2012–2013 enrollment contraction occurred at a time when institutions anticipating growth invested heavily in physical infrastructure, adding new buildings, athletic facilities, and amenities to attract new students.[9]

Unfortunately resource providers were moving in a different direction. Concerns about lagging completion rates, student debt, and college cost shifted the political mood; instead of new investments, colleges received new mandates for efficiency and accountability. Calls for accountability took on heightened fervor. The College Scorecard, designed to make the cost of a college education transparent (see https://www.whitehouse.gov/issues/education/higher-education/college-score-card), is a case in point. The federal government is rolling out a new College Rating System, which has rattled college leaders.[10] At the heart of the rating system are links between government aid and ratings on access, affordability, and student outcomes metrics. For institutions and leaders the message is clear: Change is constant, it happens quickly, and it is not predictable.

TURBULENCE AND COMPLEXITY

Turbulence and *complexity* are watchwords for today's leaders. The changing landscape has put them in the unusual position of no longer being fully in control of the institutions they lead. No longer can leaders assume that actions result in predictable results. What used to be predictable is subject to sudden change and what used to be simple has morphed to a level of complexity requiring skills not learned in graduate programs or through early career experience.

A does not necessarily lead to B because of the influence of outside forces. For example, budget cuts in midyear requiring quick responses have become increasingly common,[11] and acts of violence on campus that take over institutions and leaders have residual effects lasting long after their occurrence.[12] Turbulence and complexity are embedded in the DNA of modern organizations. They are the starting point for a new vision of leadership in community colleges.

Turbulence

Leading a college in a period of dynamic change is a difficult proposition at best. The job of leaders is more difficult, however, when the pace of change exceeds the institution's capacity to respond. Control is lost, as is the confidence that comes from practiced responses. There are no quick fixes in a turbulent landscape.

Think about your personal tendencies as a leader. What would you do upon encountering a sudden, unanticipated change? Tread carefully? Get ahead of the change? Copy the behavior of competitors? Or something else? Change is a moving target; it does not wait for institutions and leaders to catch up. There is no substitute for the experience of managing change in the real world, but we can approximate it by presenting scenarios that leaders might face in the future. We call these scenarios "what ifs."

Leaders and the Future: What if . . .

Look at your college. Consider the initiatives that have been launched recently. Look at the issues that are commanding attention. Think about the future and your college's ability to shape that future. Ask yourself:

Do faculty and staff have an understanding of forces that could impact the college? Are they alert to the dangers posed by new, unconventional competitors? Do they think about current and future threats to our current mode of operation? Do they possess an urgency about change?

Now ask yourself: Am I as a leader functioning as an architect to design what the college needs to look like tomorrow, or am I a manager keeping the college running smoothly today? Do I devote more energy to managing the present than to creating the future? Am I able to shift my attention from the present to the future and envision what is out there on the horizon?

These are not rhetorical questions. Get a pencil and rate your readiness, and your college's preparedness, for events and conditions that could radically alter the landscape.

Not prepared   *   *   *   *   *   Highly prepared

In a quest for autonomy and new resources, community colleges opt out of state systems.

Not prepared   *   *   *   *   *   Highly prepared

Community colleges eliminate academic programs and support services to free up resources for pressing infrastructure needs (facilities modernization, new technology, etc.).

Not prepared   *   *   *   *   *   Highly prepared

Funding from state and federal agencies becomes exclusively performance-driven keyed to indicators beyond completion (relationship of job to curriculum, job performance, etc.).

Not prepared   *   *   *   *   *   Highly prepared

To facilitate access and reduce student debt, community colleges institute policies enabling learners to forgo upfront tuition payments in exchange for a portion of their earnings following completion.

Not prepared   *   *   *   *   *   Highly prepared

Finding that smaller is better in terms of quality, community colleges adopt a business model predicated on mission compression, enrollment contraction, and value-based budgeting.

Not prepared   *   *   *   *   *   Highly prepared

Full-time instructors leave community colleges to form private teaching cartels delivering modularized training customized to employer needs.

Not prepared   *   *   *   *   *   Highly prepared

For-profit organizations take on functions (job placement, skills certification, data mining, etc.) poorly performed by community colleges.

Not prepared   *   *   *   *   *   Highly prepared

To increase speed and flexibility, community colleges restructure the organization into operating units each responsible for generating its own revenue.

Not prepared   *   *   *   *   *   Highly prepared

The structure of networks a college belongs to become more important for achieving operating objectives than the structure of the college itself.

Not prepared   *   *   *   *   *   Highly prepared

Employers become a key force in program and curriculum development by partnering with instructors in all facets of curriculum planning and course preparation.

Not prepared   *   *   *   *   *   Highly prepared

Proficiency takes the place of grades as the primary measure of student academic performance.

Not prepared   *   *   *   *   *   Highly prepared

The majority of teaching in community colleges moves to online or hybrid.

Not prepared   *   *   *   *   *   Highly prepared

The fifteen-week class becomes a dinosaur as instruction goes modular and students learn through modular content.

Not prepared   *   *   *   *   *   Highly prepared

Faculty autonomy becomes a relic of the past; instructors are mandated to customize course content and pedagogy to the needs of learners and receiving organizations.

Not prepared   *   *   *   *   *   Highly prepared

Bold new programs are implemented to connect part-time instructors to the center of the institution; the designation "part-time" is changed to "core" instructors.

Not prepared   *   *   *   *   *   Highly prepared

A growing number of leaders come to community colleges from outside education—a result of graduate education programs of questionable quality and relevance and marginal early career experience.

Not prepared   *   *   *   *   *   Highly prepared

Special academies for leader preparation emerge in the form of for-profit companies offering a unique learning experience certified by college governing boards.

If your marks fell somewhere in the middle, or to the left, your college may be trapped in the present and not working toward the future. Not convinced? Ask yourself three questions and do not hedge on the answers.

First, how much of your time is spent on internal rather than external challenges—managing staff, for example, in contrast to understanding the implications of new technology for teaching and learning?

Second, of the time spent looking outward, how much is spent considering how the landscape could be different in five to ten years as opposed to worrying about how to respond to a nearby competitor's technology move?

Third, of the time devoted to looking outward, how much of it is spent in consultation with faculty and staff to build common knowledge and a deeply shared view of the future?

If it is not the future, what is occupying leaders' attention? Simply two issues—resources and competitive positioning. Enrollment and resources clearly are important matters, but these foci have more to do with managing today's business than creating tomorrow's institution. Neither is more important than envisioning the future of an institution in a turbulent landscape. Neither will ensure continued success if a college fails to shape its business model to fit the landscape of the future.

A college that succeeds at stabilizing its competitive position, but fails to create a vision of what it should look like to perform at an optimal level, will find itself on a treadmill in yesterday's business model and just one step ahead of oblivion. True, the first job of leaders is to keep the ship afloat, but thinking that turbulence will be short-lived and that it can be weathered is foolhardy.

Complexity

In fast-growing organizations like community colleges, complexity generally takes two forms: evolution from a self-contained organization into a network and expansion of competition through the entry of new players. Colleges that used to be boundaried and discrete are now embedded in a network of organizations connected by technology. The actions of any one organization in the network impact, and are impacted by, the actions of other organizations.

Networks require a different approach to business—both by leaders and institutions. Leaders need to carefully consider their social capital and how they can leverage it to advance the network. Colleges need to be razor-sharp about their core mission to select partners effectively.

Networks offer advantages. The capability of network partners can be used to ward off competition from unexpected sources. Consider, for example, the entry of universities into the business of dual enrollment, online programs, and the development of online education resources such as massive online open courses (MOOCs). For decades, community colleges fueled growth through open access and low cost. Community colleges were at the vanguard of offering dual enrollment and online courses.[13] This advantage has been eroded by big-brand universities moving into the MOOC game early and racing to certify credits and degrees via online learning. Because of their size and prestige, universities have the potential to turn the enrollment market upside down and cause considerable collateral damage to latecomers like community colleges.

Complexity is much more, however, than change caused by the evolution of networks and new rules of competition. Its real impact on community colleges is in the domain of predictability. Planning has been replaced by just-in-time decision making to keep pace with environmental forces that are an amalgam of interconnected events.[14] Leaders and staff no longer have time to plan for the future nor are they able to comprehend all of the forces at work in a decision context, a circumstance that alters the way they interact with the environment.

The 2008 financial meltdown offers a poignant illustration of the effect of multiple, simultaneously occurring elements on leader comprehension and decision making. After the fact, the meltdown could be traced to numerous discrete, but interconnected events: the relaxation of banking regulations, the invention of instruments that allowed lenders to shift risk off their balance sheets, monetary policies that kept interest rates low, the evaporation of reasonable credit standards and conventional down-payment requirements, and ignorance on the part of borrowers. Leading up to the meltdown, industry leaders could see some of these elements, but no one could see them all or anticipate their consequences. The complexity of this crisis serves as a good example of the here and now and what is to come.

Complexity exceeds the cognitive limits of leaders in a landscape marked by rapidly developing, simultaneously occurring events, the consequences of which defy comprehension. Consider, for example, the confluence of forces that have brought community colleges to the threshold of transformation. Five discrete but interconnected events—*soaring cost, changing demand, declining resources, intensifying accountability,* and *disruptive technology*—have pushed leaders to rethink their historic business model. These forces are universally acknowledged, but their consequences and the manner in which they will play out over the long term are not fully understood. In a simple world, the relationship of events fueling transformation could be described as follows:

> Whereas the price of products and services in many sectors has fallen dramatically, colleges and universities have charged more for the same level of service.[15] For most students, the return on investment remains favorable,[16] but for those who have gone deep into debt it is not value for the money. More money is being invested in the same value—an imbalance caused by declining government support and labor market innovation that has altered the economic benefit of higher education. By themselves, these events would generate change although it would be incremental. An additional event—advancing technology—ensures change will happen. The Internet, which has turned businesses from newspapers to music to retail upside down, could upend colleges committed to a traditional business model. Online education resources are rapidly changing education content and delivery, and this innovation will be a key catalyst in the cycle of disruptive innovation leading to transformation.

Describing the overall organizational challenge is easy, but the devil is in the details. Is it possible for leaders to get their arms around the interaction of simultaneously occurring events and comprehend their long-term consequences? Research indicates that it is difficult, if not impossible, for individual decision makers to see all of the forces at work at one time in a turbulent environment.[17]

What if leaders believe they can absorb and make sense of more information than they actually can? Will they act prematurely and make decisions without fully comprehending their consequences? Or will they wait too long to react and miss opportunities? Research and practice have much to tell us about navigating complexity in a turbulent environment,[18] but this knowledge seems not to have permeated the thinking of today's leaders or the programs that prepare them.

CONSTRUCTS OF TRANSFORMATION

The time has come to think of transformation as an era in a college's development, not an event or episode. When leaders conceive of transformation in this way they understand and manage it differently. Quick fixes give way to minding the core purpose, and holding with tradition gives way to thinking in new ways. Leaders who think differently are able to connect the dots between competing forces and recognize that community colleges as organizations must change on a large scale. Part and parcel of connecting the dots is understanding core constructs in organizational change.

Organizational Change

In simple terms, organizational change is the act of modifying structures, systems, and processes to stay ahead of competitors. A college's change drivers include the leader's vision, the competitive environment, student demand, economic conditions, information technology, and government policy actions. By reshaping how colleges operate and how they compete with one another, information technology has become the single most powerful force in organizational change.[19]

Staggering amounts of information are now available to organizations—from proprietary big data to public sources of open data. Fast-moving, for-profit competitors are particularly adept at using information technology to create advantage. Their strategy is simple: inject a learning platform between traditional institutions and learners using processing and analytical capabilities in combination with smart mobile devices to create alternatives for learners.[20] To compete with unconventional rivals, community colleges will have no choice but to challenge their assumptions and embrace change—hence the mantra "change or die."

Digitization

Digitization, the process of converting information into a digital format that can be organized into discrete units of data that devices with computing capacity can process and store,[21] makes information easier to preserve, access, and share. It eradicates barriers to market entry for start-up organizations. Think of the University of Phoenix and their leveraging of technology to deliver online programming at scale. No longer is education content the sole domain of brick-and-mortar institutions.

In fact, the plug-and-play nature of digital information today enables learners to conveniently access information at low or no cost.[22] In so doing, ready access to digital information disrupts traditional delivery systems and creates openings for focused, fast-moving competitors. New market entrants can scale up quickly and offer education at a lower cost than community colleges, and these new entrants can grow rapidly as learners flock to a superior product at a competitive cost. Think Western Governors University (WGU) and their promise of an accredited, competency-based degree with little to no college debt; they now serve fifty thousand students in fifty states.

By contrast, established institutions typically respond by accelerating technology investment, and in so doing, they push the rate of internal adoption to a tipping point.[23] When this happens, adopters outnumber resisters, and what was once radical becomes normal. Institutions that embrace digitization maintain market share, whereas slow-to-adopt institutions have little choice but to change quickly or lose market share.

Historically, in the diffusion of innovation,[24] early technology adopters have represented a distinct minority. Not until more join the bandwagon does technology acceptance occur. There is a clear advantage to being on the forward edge of adoption, especially in a crowded market. Laggards to adoption spend heavily on technology but experience diminishing return as early adopters become proficient with advanced technology and gobble up market share. The key for leaders and institutions is to anticipate and get in front of change, assess strategic options, and move quickly.

Sustaining and Disrupting Innovation

In every market there is a trajectory of performance improvement that consumers can absorb and use. Some consumers are demanding; they expect more and better service and will pay for it. Others seek lower cost and will accept modest improvement. *Sustaining innovations* move the scope and quality of service up the performance ladder by making current services better without changing the rules of the game.

Research has shown, however, that as organizations improve their service and elevate cost, they eventually outstrip the ability of customers to receive benefit from the improvement.[25] In higher education, this scenario would be analogous to improving curricula and support services through technology investment, and then increasing tuition and fees to pay for this new technology without bringing added value and benefit to learners.

The disconnect between the scope and quality of service and the value-add for learners opens up an opportunity for *disruptive innovation*.[26] Disruptive innovation changes the rules of the game by bringing radical new offerings to current customers. As previously noted, scalable technology in the form of online learning is an example of an innovation that has disrupted the status quo and will continue to disrupt community colleges and other low-cost providers by carrying the business model of lower-cost teaching universities upstream and high-cost research universities downstream to learners.

Business Model

A business model describes the rationale of how an organization creates and delivers value to its customers. It represent core aspects of a business, including purpose, target audiences, service offerings, organizational structure, systems and operating processes, and policies. Historically, business models were organized into two basic types: "pipes" and "platforms."[27] Pipes create products and services, push them out, and sell them downstream to customers. There is a linear flow, much like water flowing through a pipe. Unlike pipes, platforms do more than simply create and push products and services to customers. "They enable customers to create and consume value."[28]

The platform provides a means to create, extend, and use information. The users create the value for the product versus the product having value in and of itself. An example of a platform is YouTube. Students and faculty put up video content on YouTube that others can view; for example, as an online education resource that is independent of a formal course. Financial value is created for colleges by charging for the certification and credentialing of content.[29]

In higher education, there are three generic types of business models as defined by Christensen:[30] solution shops, value-adding process businesses, and facilitated user networks. Each is comprised of its own value proposition, processes, and resources. Community colleges are an amalgam of all three types, which is a distinguishing feature of their organizational architecture.

Solution shops are focused on diagnosing and solving problems. An example of a solution shop would be the outreach function of community colleges working with P–12 schools to address basic skills deficiencies in elementary and middle school students. Organizations with value-adding business models focus on customers that are incomplete or unfinished. They use organizational resources and processes to transform them into more complete outputs of higher value.

The teaching function of a community college is congruous with this model, particularly as students complete courses and programs that deliver market skills. Finally, the facilitated user network is an enterprise in which learners exchange knowledge and skills with one another. The workforce development function of a community college represents a facilitated network in which employers and institutions collaborate to prepare trained workers.

Despite their best intentions, organizations that embrace multiple business models have costly overhead, not because of management inefficiencies, but because it is difficult to resource and manage the resulting complexity. The dilemma of how to create business efficiencies while pursuing innovation invariably leads to a conundrum. This is exactly the plight of community colleges today, and it underscores the importance and necessity of their quest for new business models.

Transformation

Organizational transformation is a form of quantum change involving radical, fundamental change in an organization's mission, strategy, structure, systems, and culture—in contrast to incremental improvement.[31] Unlike incremental change, which implies forward progress on the same trajectory, transformation implies a basic change of character and little or no resemblance to past configuration or structure.[32] An example of transformation would be changing an institution's structure and culture from a traditional top-down hierarchy to self-directing teams. Examples of incremental improvement would include implementation of new technology to improve efficiency or continuous improvement as a quality management process.

Deep organizational change almost always requires a burning platform, of which there are two kinds: *reactive* and *proactive*.[33] A reactive platform involves leaders waiting until a situation has become critical and then responding reactively by reorganizing, changing leadership, downsizing, consolidating functions and systems, or implementing aggressive cost-cutting measures without understanding the end effects of these decisions. Most leaders do not stay in position long enough to directly experience the long-term consequences of reactive change. Change of this type has institution-wide effects that span multiple units and may impact a college's operations for years to come. This may explain why so many leaders do not learn from experience. When the consequences of a decision are removed from the process of making a decision, the potential for learning is lost. Furthermore, leaders are often conditioned to plan for, and focus on, the future.

In this book we advocate generative thinking, the process of framing problems from multiple perspectives and making sense of ambiguous situations, which requires that leaders explore and reinterpret the past to find "new ways of framing old problems, and new sources of ideas.[34] "Reactive change *does not* lead to organizational transformation."[35] People get comfortable with the way things are done and are reluctant to face potential failure. The mental maps guiding their actions are ingrained and tough to change, which is a circumstance that does little to lift institutions.[36]

A *proactive* burning platform occurs when leaders realize that although forces in the external environment may not have reached a critical stage, they will reach that point if a sense of urgency does not develop regarding how the institution conducts business. Proactive leaders define a new direction, build a sense of urgency, and reconfigure the organization through change that realigns structures, systems, and resources around a new mission or strategy that increases the value delivered to customers.[37] Proactive change *does lead* to organizational transformation because it involves questioning long-held beliefs and assumptions about how colleges should operate.[38]

Reinvention

Reinvention is a form of change involving replacement of systems, structures, and processes currently in place with something new or different. It signals a point in time when organizations are ready to let go of the past and to start anew.[39] Wikipedia and other readily available online resources that have replaced hard-copy encyclopedias serve as a good example of reinvention.

Organizations that are successful at reinvention typically possess committed leaders, a deep sense of trust among employees, and the courage to eliminate practices that have outlived their utility. They pursue lofty goals and a results-oriented culture. These organizations typically embrace multiple ways of thinking and doing. Collaboration among staff with different backgrounds, managerial styles, and expertise is valued throughout the organization. Kotter's[40] description of organizations with a "dual operating system" comprised of a network structure operating side by side with the hierarchy is an excellent example of reinvention. There is a healthy balance between resources allocated to current operations and those earmarked for long-term development.

FROM IMPROVEMENT TO TRANSFORMATION

Continuous improvement is necessary and important, but it will not turn an average institution into a high performer. A select group of community colleges have won the Aspen Prize for Excellence, which is an award for better or best, not different. By now you know the answers to these questions: Did the prize winners operate in ways that were fundamentally different from other colleges, or did they simply do things better? How much would it help them to become even better at doing what they already do well? Would it enable them to increase market share or to acquire new revenue streams? The point is simple. In the future it will not be enough for a college to get better at what it is already doing, as important as this might be. A college will need to be capable of fundamentally reconceiving itself, regenerating its core vision, and ultimately reinventing itself within the higher education industry. In short, a college will need to be capable of metamorphosis.

The transformation challenge facing community colleges is, for the most part, a result of the failure of institutions to reinvent their core vision over the past decade. Education leaders are looking for new business models because they have surrendered industry leadership to fast-moving, for-profit start-ups and to traditional institutions that have been successful at regeneration. Think about Southern New Hampshire University, which today is aggressively capturing new online markets; its business model bears little resemblance to that of the institution that was founded in Manchester in 1932.

Take community colleges and MOOCs as another example. Although industry experts initially assumed that community colleges had the right kind of organization, expertise, and personnel to capture key segments of the MOOC market, such observations missed a deeper point. The real issue was not that community colleges had the right kind of organization, but that they moved too slowly to capture the MOOC wave that was reshaping the market.

For much of the past decade, community colleges have continued to rely on a time-tested strategy of open access, local convenience, and low cost to maintain market advantage. This strategy amounts to driving toward the future while looking out the rearview mirror. By the time leaders looked up and realized that the MOOC and, more generally, the online education resource train had left the station, universities and for-profits had carved out market share and seized the initiative.

Initiating and managing the task of transformation can energize a college and make it move faster; it cannot, however, turn a college into an industry leader. To become a leader, a college must have a point of view about where the higher education industry is going and get there ahead of competitors. This perspective prompts us to ask how much energy community colleges are spending on catching up with industry leaders, in contrast to reinventing the industry.

Although transformation is on the management agenda of most colleges, we believe that to create the future, a college must also be capable of transformation. By transforming itself, a college contributes to the reinvention of the industry. And leadership must be reinvented to succeed in the new industry. In our view, a principal task for community colleges going forward will be to transform higher education, not simply to perform better within it. To accomplish this, these colleges will need leaders who are expert at generative thinking, and who deeply understand and appreciate the differences between improvement and transformation.

Transformation is easier said than done. It begins with the question: "Transform to what?" A transformation agenda does not mean much unless it is driven by a point of view of what higher education will look like in the future. What forces will drive the industry? What will leaders need to do to ensure that an institution develops in a way that positions it in front of the industry? What skills and capabilities must leaders possess to enable a college to occupy the industry high ground in the future? A point of view about the future shape of higher education enables a college to create a proactive agenda for transformation.

How does this happen? Let us move from organizational lingo to the real world in which colleges compete for market share and talent. It was a particular point of view about the future direction of higher education that inspired pioneering leaders to establish open-access, low-cost institutions—community colleges—more than a century ago, and it was insight into the rapidly changing world of information technology that led MIT in spring 2001 to announce that the content of virtually all of its courses would be posted on the Web and available to teachers and students around the world free of charge. MIT's OpenCourseWare changed the industry of higher education by placing course content in the hands of anyone, anytime, anywhere.

Likewise, the University of Wisconsin's understanding of technology and youth learning preferences provided the impetus for curtailing the use of fifteen-week classes in their MBA Consortium to deliver instructional content. Instead, they opted to split course work into online modules (see http://www.wisconsinonlinemba.org/mba/modules.php). This modular format is exactly what our European counterparts are doing through open educational borders via the Bologna Declaration.

Industry foresight is not limited to colleges and universities. Knowing that employers are concerned about skill deficits and that community colleges are struggling to make the connection between education and work, WorkAmerica changed the education–work compact by partnering directly with employers to deliver legally binding job offers to learners before enrollment at a partner college (see http://www.workamerica.co/).

Workforce IO followed suit with a program certifying skill attainment to employers by awarding badges to students, certifying attainment of valued job skills. By inserting themselves between colleges and employers, WorkAmerica and Workforce IO bolstered the economic return of college attendance by ensuring a tighter connection between education and work.

Transformation is an imperative for *every* college. The real issue is not whether or not it will happen but *when* it will happen. There are important questions to consider leading up to transformation: Does it happen belatedly in a crisis atmosphere or with foresight in a rational and deliberate atmosphere? Is the transformation agenda motivated and set by fast-moving competitors or by a college's insight into the future? Is transformation episodic or continual, and is it within the purview of leaders or embraced by staff throughout the organization? However lean and agile a college, it still needs strong leadership. But the leadership we envision is not exclusively at the top of a college. It is an amalgamation of the collective intelligence and imagination of faculty and staff throughout the college who must possess an understanding of the industry and an enlightened view of what it means to transform.

This book is as much about how to implant this view of leadership as it is about developing the next generation of leaders for colleges engaged in the business of transformation.

NOTES

1. David Schwen, "College, Reinvented," *Chronicle of Higher Education*, October 15, 2012.

2. Amanda M. Fairbanks, "Peter Thiel Awards $100,000 to Entrepreneurs Under 20." *The Huffington Post*, May 25, 2011, http://www.huffingtonpost.com/2011/05/25/peter-thiel-fellowship_n_867134.html.

3. "The Digital Degree," *The Economist*, June 28, 2014, ¶ 1, http://www.economist.com/news/briefing/21605899-staid-higher-education-business-about-experience-welcome-earthquake-digital.

4. Mark Schneider and Lu Yin, *The Hidden Costs of Community Colleges* (Washington, DC: American Institutes for Research, 2011).

5. Teresa A. Sullivan, Christopher Mackie, William F. Massy, and Esha Shinyha, eds., *Improving Measurement of Productivity in Higher Education* (Washington, DC: National Academies Press, 2012).

6. Cejda and Murray, eds., *Hiring the Next Generation of Faculty.*

7. Richard Alfred, "Leaders, Leveraging, and Abundance: Competencies for the Future," 109–120.

8. Richard Perez-Pena, "College Enrollment Falls as Economy Recovers," *The New York Times*, July 25, 2013, http://www.nytimes.com/2013/07/26/

education/in-a-recovering-economy-a-decline-in-college-enrollment.html? pagewanted=all&_r=2&.

9. Jon Marcus, "Despite Massive Budget Cuts, There's a Building Boom in U.S. Higher Education," *The Hechinger Report*, April 2, 2012, http://hechinger report.org/content/despite-massive-budget-cuts-theres-a-building-boom-in-u-s-higher-education_8219/.

10. Michael D. Shear, "Colleges Rattled as Obama Seeks Rating System," *The New York Times*, May 25, 2014, http://www.nytimes.com/2014/05/26/us/colleges-rattled-as-obama-presses-rating-system.html?_r=0.

11. Scott Jaschik, "Outlook for Community Colleges," *Inside Higher Ed*, November 8, 2013, https://www.insidehighered.com/news/2013/11/08/survey-finds-mixed-outlook-community-colleges.

12. Greg Botelho and Chandler Friedman, "Police: Student Shot 2 Women at Virginia Community College before Being Subdued," *CNN*, April 12, 2013, http://www.cnn.com/2013/04/12/us/virginia-community-college-shooting/.

13. I. Elaine Allen and Jeff Seaman, "Changing Course: Ten Years of Tracking Online Education in the United States," (Sloan Consortium and Pearson, January 2013), http://www.onlinelearningsurvey.com/reports/changingcourse.pdf.

14. Harvard Business Review, *Making Smart Decisions* (Boston: Harvard Business School Publishing Corporation, 2011).

15. Robert B. Archibald and David H. Feldman, *Why Does College Cost So Much?* (New York: Oxford University Press, 2011).

16. Sandy Baum, Jennifer Ma, and Kathleen Payea, "Education Pays 2010: The Benefits of Higher Education for Individual and Society," (College Board Advocacy and Policy Center, 2010), http://trends.collegeboard.org/sites/default/files/education-pays-2010-full-report.pdf.

17. Kevin Kelly and Gary E. Hayes, *Leading in Turbulent Times* (San Francisco: Berrett-Koehler Publishers, Inc., 2010).

18. Kelly and Hayes, *Leading in Turbulent Times.*

19. Suzanne Rivard, Benoit Aubert, Michel Patry, Guy Pare, and Heather A. Smith, *Information Technology and Organizational Transformation: Solving the Management Puzzle* (New York: Routledge, 2004).

20. Martin Hirt and Paul Wilmott, "Strategic Principles for Competing in the Digital Age," *McKinsey Quarterly (May 22, 2014)*, http://www.mckinsey.com/insights/strategy/strategic_principles_for_competing_in_the_digital_age.

21. Lorna M. Hughes, *Digitizing Collections: Strategic Issues for the Information Manager* (London, England: Facet, 2004).

22. Tomayess Issa, Pedro Isaisa, and Piet Kommers, *Multicultural Awareness and Technology in Higher Education: Global Perspective* (Hershey, PA: Information Science Reference, 2014).

23. Malcolm Gladwell, *The Tipping Point: How Little Things Can Make a Big Difference* (Boston: Little, Brown and Company, 2000).

24. Everett M. Rogers, *Diffusion of Innovations,* 5th ed. (New York: Free Press, 2003).

25. Clayton M. Christensen and Michael E. Raynor, *The Innovator's Solution: Creating and Sustaining Successful Growth.* (Boston: Harvard Business School Publishing Corporation, 2003).

26. Clayton Christensen, "Disruptive Innovation and Catalytic Change," *Futures Forum, Harvard Business School* (2008): 43–46.

27. Sangeet Paul Choudary, "Why Business Models Fail: Pipes vs. Platforms," *Wired,* October 21, 2013, ¶ 2, http://www.wired.com/2013/10/why-business-models-fail-pipes-vs-platforms/.

28. Choudary, "Why Business Models," ¶ 2.

29. Issa, Isaisa, and Kommers, *Multicultural Awareness.*

30. Christensen, "Disruptive Innovation."

31. Karen Martin and Mike Osterling, *Value Stream Mapping: How to Visualize Work and Align Leadership for Organizational Transformation* (New York: McGraw-Hill, 2013).

32. Adrianna Kezar, *How Colleges Change: Understanding, Leading, and Enacting Change* (New York: Routledge, 2013).

33. Mark Bodnarczuk, "What Is Organizational Transformation and Should You Transform?" *Ezine Articles,* March 8, 2012, http://ezinearticles.com/?What-Is-Organizational-Transformation-and-Should-You-Transform?&id=6927072.

34. William Ryan, Richard Chait, and Barbara Taylor, "Governance as Leadership: Bringing New Governing Mindsets to Old Challenges," *Board Source,* 2008, http://www.michaeldavidson.biz/downloads/Leadership.pdf, ¶ 4.

35. Bodnarczuk, "Organizational Transformation," ¶ 4.

36. Peter M. Senge, *The Fifth Discipline* (New York: Currency/Doubleday, 1990).

37. John P. Kotter, *Leading Change* (Boston: Harvard Business Review Press, 2012).

38. Peter Eckel and Adrianna Kezar, "The Challenges Facing Academic Decision Making: Contemporary Issues and Steadfast Structures," in *The Shifting Frontiers of Academic Decision Making: Responding to New Priorities, Creating New Pathways,* ed. Peter Eckel (Washington, DC: American Council on Education/Oryx Press Series on Higher Education, 2006), 1–15.

39. Josh Linkner, *The Road to Reinvention: How to Drive Disruption and Accelerate Transformation* (San Francisco: Jossey-Bass, 2014).

40. John P. Kotter, *Accelerate: Building Strategic Agility for a Faster-Moving World* (Boston: Harvard Business Review Press, 2014), 12.

3

LEADING THE TRANSFORMATION

Even a grand vision and agenda will fall flat if an organization's people lack a shared mindset and commitment. And it takes the right culture and talent to drive and sustain change.

—Andrew Dyer, Grant Freeland, Steve Gunby, and Cynthia DeTar[1]

The fast-changing landscape and the challenge it poses to organizations has put transformation on the radar screen of college and university leaders, most of whom are acutely aware that old business models will be woefully inadequate for success in this new environment.

In a 2014 survey of campus leaders by the *Chronicle of Higher Education*, more than half of the responding presidents indicated a need for at least "a moderate amount of disruption" in higher education. Two-thirds indicated that the industry will look different ten years from now than it does today, suggesting growing awareness of problems with an outmoded business model and a belief that evolutionary change will not be sufficient to promote growth and vitality.[2]

The transformation of our colleges from the inside out is a challenge that every leader will face. And the road to a constantly shifting destination will be anything but smooth. For community colleges, this road will run through organizational culture and values. The next generation of leaders will need to read culture, gauge the entrenched interests of constituencies, and adeptly adjust culture and values to succeed in the increasingly unfamiliar landscape of higher education.

Having reached a point of recognition that transformation will be part of every institution's development agenda, how can leaders organize and manage the journey in the unique organizational environment that is the community college? The ready answer is that leaders who pursue transformation would be well advised to become familiar with methodologies and models for managing transformation that have been adopted and successfully used by organizations both inside and outside education. There are numerous models, and whether it's a five-, ten-, or twelve-step model for change, basic change management principles are involved and they provide a sound foundation for engaging in what can be tricky, sometimes treacherous, work.

A model for transformation with particular utility for community colleges is adopted from a theory of leadership for the transformation of health-care organizations posited by Reinertsen in 2004.[3] This model incorporates the experience of transformational change in multiple industries, including Toyota in the automotive industry with guidance from W. Edwards Deming.

The writings of John Kotter[4] also inform the transformation model, along with the experience of one of our authors in leading transformation at two quite different community colleges. Although calls for transformational leadership have been more frequent of late, to date a blueprint does not exist for what leaders fundamentally must do to transform their institutions.

This chapter is intended to be a guide for community college leaders engaged in the transformation process; in particular, it provides the basics of what must be done to successfully navigate and lead institutional change.

BEGINNING THE TRANSFORMATION

Colleges and universities have repeatedly used incremental fixes to counter major challenges such as declining resources, stringent accountability mandates, and changing patterns of growth. Incremental fixes—what Christensen labels "sustaining innovations"[5]—address the palpable effects of change but not the root cause.

At the core of transformation is a shift in institutional priorities and resource allocation away *from* an overbuilt portfolio of academic programs and support services *to* measurable learning outcomes that demonstrably prepare students for gainful employment. The infrastructures and systems in place at today's colleges tend toward redundancy and inefficiency, understandably reflecting the core values of institutions that throughout most of their history have strained to be all things to all people. For these institutions, addition, in contrast to substitution or elimination, has been the primary road to change. Rooted in the open-access mission is a more-is-better approach to business.

Our colleges were designed to fuel growth by accommodating the lifelong educational needs of virtually all citizens within a small geographical footprint. "More" means more of everything—programs and services, expenditures and costs, infrastructure and facilities, part-time personnel to fill the gap between need and capacity, and resources. To succeed in the future, this approach will need to give way to a system in which business functions that add little to no value to the educational experience are pruned or distributed to network partners, resources are strategically deployed, and curricula are restructured to deliver the highest possible educational value to learners.

The first step in pursuing a change tapestry of this magnitude is to define the objective, which in this case is enhanced value for learner investment. At a college led by one of the authors of this book, transformation began with the identification of a big, organizing goal: 100 percent student success. This goal was intended to communicate a clear vision of what a transformed college would consistently deliver, a vision that could be easily understood and jointly owned by every stakeholder.

A big goal has the advantage of distilling institutional mission into a precise and simple reason for being that serves as a guiding principle for transformation. Leaders across functions are responsible for translating the goal into actionable, strategic initiatives such as agile academic portfolio management, streamlined enrollment processes, asset optimization, integrated academic and extracurricular student experiences, applied business intelligence, and so forth. The focus on a singular goal of student success is an important part of the process because it engages all employees in understanding how their individual contribution connects with the organization today and as it will exist in the future.

Providing an early glimpse of what a college will look like in a transformed state makes the big goal less fuzzy and makes clear that transformation is a long-term endeavor. One of Stephen Covey's habits for effective people is to establish a clear picture of priorities—values, goals, and high-leverage activities—and then organize around them.[6] Applied to organizations, this is exactly what is required for transformational leadership. Once a clear picture of the future is established, leaders are ready to pursue a blueprint for change.

IMPERATIVES OF TRANSFORMATION

Leaders who accept the transformation challenge will be required to succeed on multiple fronts. They will need to reframe core values, foster a capability for improvement throughout the organization, and collaborate both internally and across competitive boundaries. They will need to become adept at sensing and responding to ever-changing environmental conditions, optimizing resources, and driving system-level (and project-level) results. Success will depend on their ability to frame big goals and maintain constancy of purpose over the long and winding road of the transformational journey.

Reframe Cultural Values

A first order of business is to contrast current cultural norms with those required for a transformed college. Values, habits, and beliefs that will need to be reframed from a self-contained organization to a network organization are a prime example of the value shift that community colleges will need to embrace. This shift is best guided by leaders who clearly model and live by the new rules. For example, similar to the health-care industry and physicians, a core higher education value has been to regard educational quality as an individual or collective faculty responsibility, and therefore, to "value individual professional autonomy more highly than almost any other professional cultural attribute."[7] Yet, it is the work of the collective that must be harnessed to effect real change.

Reframing this core professional value is a *transformational* as opposed to a *transactional* task because the change must be fully incorporated into the college culture in contrast to being crafted to suit the individual. Transformational change requires leaders at all levels to "make the transformation personal, to engage others, and to spotlight successes as they emerge."[8] This is more easily said than done because changing deeply held values is one of the most difficult aspects of transformation.

Consider the example of one of the authors who met regularly with college employees, student groups, and community stakeholders upon entering a small college where student completion had dropped precipitously in preceding years and other key performance indicators were flagging. She reviewed and shared data, identified key opportunities for improvement, established a set of core messages, and then consistently communicated these messages back to the campus community in written reports, at faculty and staff meetings, and at open forums. Even in the face of resistance, the ubiquitous voice of the "customer" in highlighting what is broken can ease the employee angst that almost always accompanies organizational and operational reform.[9]

The demonstration of commitment to 100 percent student success was buttressed by shifting 25 percent of resources from administrative to academic and student support functions over a two-year period. Unnecessary, underutilized, and redundant services were eliminated, and employees were notified of the cuts as well as the rationale behind the cuts. The actions themselves, and the transparency in communicating the actions, were shocking for a culture unaccustomed to such actions or disclosures.

Once the management structure was streamlined, new investments were made in faculty development, student scholarships, and student engagement, all of which were prioritized in a board-approved strategic plan as clear needs and priorities. Functions like the library and information technology were merged to ensure college-wide access to learning resources through a fully integrated information management system.

The changes required to transform an organization cannot be brought about by leaders who are not personally committed to the process and to their own transformational journey. They must also be willing to take significant risks along the way and must make and reinforce their personal commitment to the desired future-state of the organization. Likewise, they must listen carefully to the insights and the emotions of affected employees and stakeholders, and especially students.

Illustrative "stories" should be shared, as appropriate, with the management team, faculty and staff, the board, and external stakeholders as a means of putting a face on the mandate for change. In the case of our author, such stories peppered every annual report, monthly communiqué, campus address, board presentation, and community speech.

Create "Improvement" and Leadership Capability

Most community colleges do not have large numbers of capable, trained change agents in their ranks. Although every college has early adopters and change champions, employees with extensive knowledge and training in improvement methods tend to be rare. The resulting lack of a critical mass of staff who understand change and know how to use improvement tools hinders change efforts. Capacity building in change management is best structured as just-in-time training as opposed to investing in a massive training initiative. Still, "investment in an intentional, measured plan to build and use capability is required."[10]

Leadership capability is as important as change or improvement capability. Thus, implementing employee development programs that are designed to teach leadership fundamentals can help build and deploy leaders throughout the organization and build institution-wide capacity for transformation. The presence of system-level leadership pushing a change agenda throughout the organization is particularly valuable in overcoming technical, political, and cultural barriers.

In preparation for a significant round of faculty labor negotiations, one of the authors established partnerships with neighboring universities' labor relations and business faculty, respectively, to deliver customized professional development programming focused on interest-based bargaining and shared governance. A point of contention in labor negotiations was how faculty members would engage in the development and delivery of online courses. Realizing that the absence of broadly distributed and well-informed leaders, particularly in the union ranks, would limit transformational initiatives like online programming, a carefully designed, long-term program for faculty and staff development was initiated for the express purpose of growing strategic leaders.

The resulting win for the college over the long term was a labor agreement that not only allowed for the delivery of online offerings, but also included specific terms and conditions of delivery that would prove to give the college a competitive advantage in the industry. This example demonstrates the importance of faculty engagement and leadership of instructional programs, such as online education, to move the institution forward.

This is a brief, high-level summary of what was actually a highly complex initiative that spanned several years, an initiative that admittedly had its fair share of stumbles and false starts. Still, the example is illustrative of the importance of proper training, relationship building, and shared leadership to move the change initiative past obstacles. The well-planned and carefully executed development of leaders at all levels of the organization is a necessary and critical investment of time and resources when the goal is transformation.

Development of campus staff is also important, given the fundamental need to engage talent throughout colleges that are perpetually underresourced. For example, in the course of transforming what were highly disjointed functions spread across multiple offices into a reengineered, student-centered enrollment services operation, one of the authors launched an internal certification program for mid-level managers and staff for training in project management. Project management is an essential skill for any leader seeking to effectively execute change. The breadth and depth of change required for transformation simply cannot be executed by an individual or group not well versed in project management.

The sheer magnitude and pace of change will strain even the best leaders and leadership teams. As change commences on multiple fronts, weaknesses in current systems are exposed, as are leader shortcomings in areas such as communication, project management, and business intelligence. Skill development at the level of project management and organizational management requires forethought and comprehensive planning for targeted professional development and leadership training.

Sense and Respond

All leaders need clear lines of sight across their portfolio of programs and services—their objectives, service markets, resources, and performance. Beyond college walls, they need the skills and the discipline to envision how the industry will evolve. They must stand ready to alter plans and operations in light of market shifts, fluctuating resources, and leadership transitions.

A flexible organizational architecture is necessary for innovation and the business model must be fluid to allow for rapid asset reallocation in response to market changes. Opportunism and entrepreneurialism will be core competencies for the new generation of community college leaders who will gain competitive advantage by delivering new or repackaged programs and services faster, cheaper, and on demand.

Building a capability for sensing and responding to market changes will be at the heart of institutional strategy in tomorrow's community colleges. This can only be accomplished if an infrastructure is in place for data collection, assessment, and continuous improvement. As part of a transformation initiative at a large northeastern community college, one of our authors married a comprehensive reorganization plan directly to accrediting standards in an effort to keep the institution focused on quality improvement in support of student success as a singular goal and to reduce redundancy in data systems and reporting.

Clean and usable data across operations were viewed as essential—an outcome that would only be possible through investment in institutional research and technology. Institutional research underwent a metamorphosis, changing from a compliance-reporting to a central-intelligence function. Strategic plan target goals and measurable objectives were carefully cross-walked to accreditation standards.

Next, extensive training in the planning and assessment methodology was provided for faculty, staff, and administrative users, and a platform for managing planning and assessment processes (WEAVEonline™) was adopted and used to monitor improvement across functions. Over time, whole functions, positions, and programs were eliminated on the basis of carefully executed assessments, and new functions, positions, and programs were added through the same process.

Institutional policies and procedures were reviewed and, in many cases, rewritten to align with and support new ways of doing business.

Further, a new policy was developed to require regular and systematic review of all institutional policies to guard against quick fixes as a way of doing business and to accommodate new business practices and processes going forward. Anticipating and building carefully designed systems that directly support an exceptional student experience and, at the same time, fluid environmental conditions will emerge as a hallmark of effective leadership at community colleges.

Community colleges are complex organizations, to be sure, but colleges cannot afford to fly blind. The strategic importance of all programs and services, and each and every institutional asset, must be continuously assessed relative to the core mission and goals of the college. Data will be increasingly critical to this management function, and big-data techniques are calling into question even the most common management theories, such as the 80–20 rule that assumes that if an organization is 80 percent efficient, that is the best one can hope to achieve.

With a fully functioning system for data collection and management, it has become relatively easy to conduct trial-and-error testing of small-scale operations to squeeze out the remaining 20 percent of improvement. "Organizations accustomed to doing things the old way may find it hard to recognize that it is worth investing in testing and data analysis," but like natural selection, ongoing small improvements in an organization can yield long-term competitiveness and sustainability.[11]

Collaborate across Competitive Boundaries

Collaboration across sectors is necessary to create an environment that simultaneously delivers business results and community benefit. Working in isolation from the larger P–12 and higher education communities will impede transformation. Student progress toward educational and career goals is stymied by fragmentation as is evidenced by the large number of students who are moving between institutions and failing to obtain a credential because of failed or nonexistent cross-institutional collaboration.

Collaboration reduces unnecessary cost and duplication of effort for common industry procedures such as admissions and financial aid. Universal course standards, systematic advisement within and across institutions, and seamless pathways to a degree are industry processes that must be addressed by transformation leaders across sectors. Even before the federal government finalizes its college ratings plan for public performance reporting, leaders would do well to begin to collaborate across competitive boundaries toward the goal of furthering student success.

Collaboration is not a natural act for those leaders who are competitive by nature and unaccustomed to cross-institutional teamwork. However, the benefits that can be realized through collaboration are limitless. In fact, no leader's transformation journey will be complete without a substantial investment in collaboration. Don't buy it? Look at your college's budget and ask yourself how much of your portfolio of programs and services could be delivered without the support of network partners.

Connections also need to be made with business and industry partners, which can create considerable budget flexibility. Although the relationship between business results and benefit to the community may be difficult to establish outside of economic impact reports, colleges that squander resources through questionable practices simply cannot effectively contribute to community well-being. Leaders interested in community development—an increasingly important role in communities undergoing upheaval—have no choice but to open themselves to new ways of doing business and to building cultures that embrace change. A college that gets ahead of the change curve has a better chance of bringing a community along with it in the journey toward optimal health and well-being.

Optimize Resources and Drive System-Level Results

The disruptive forces confronting community colleges today have caused a shift from a landscape of known problems and solutions to one replete with unknowns. Savvy, visionary leaders know that current tools for managing risk and leveraging assets may not work in this new landscape. These leaders are beginning to reshape operations and resources in ways that leverage assets and mitigate risk relative to achieving the core educational mission.

One strategy that high-performing colleges are using to make this shift is resource sharing across basic business operations such as information technology, human resources, and property management. The State University of New York, for example, has set as a priority goal the expansion of shared, multicampus business functions and services as a means of leveraging assets more wisely in support of educational quality.[12] Given the unique nature of colleges and universities, sharing business operations across multiple colleges is often more cost effective and more easily managed than outsourcing, which in the past several decades has become common practice across a wide range of services.

Outsourcing food services, payroll, student housing, and book-stores—and the positions associated with those functions—has become a standard practice in community colleges, but outsourcing faculty is something of a game changer. Because education is a labor-intensive industry, personnel costs generally account for upward of 80 percent of expenditures, so tackling these costs head-on cannot be avoided.

In Michigan, a growing number of community colleges are turning the recruitment and hiring of adjunct instructors over to educational staffing companies such as EDUStaff. In 2014, Jackson College successfully negotiated a transfer of adjunct hiring and payroll services to EDUStaff as part of a collective bargaining agreement—a move that is being closely watched by faculty who are concerned about the potential impact on "instruction, students and professional relationships."[13]

Given the time and resources required for the selection and hiring of qualified part-time faculty and the rising cost of benefits for full-time employees, privatization of instructional staff—part-time and full-time—will likely become more common in the future, providing leaders with an opportunity to reduce costs while simultaneously shaping the instructional workforce in ways that align with college priorities and, at the same time, optimize flexibility.

In addition to off-loading administrative processes that add little to the core mission and rethinking how to resource instructional staffing, leaders will be required to infuse smart technology or artificial intelligence into the talent equation. For leaders who are able to operate across a wide range of intertwined capabilities, talent management presents a significant opportunity for innovation, but talent management is no longer limited to managing people.

Assembling the right mix of human talent and smart technologies and applying these resources to student learning outcomes will be one of the

greatest challenges and most promising of opportunities for the transformational leader. The cultivation of agile organizations that anticipate
and respond to changing market conditions requires a deliberate and
methodical approach to identifying faculty and staff who possess, in addition to technical skills, business acumen, a passion for innovation, and
a commitment to mission—perhaps the only constant across workplace
generations in community colleges. However, striking the right balance
between human and technological resources, and rethinking roles and
responsibilities of employees relative to technology will be required of
all leaders in the future.

Driving system-level results is best accomplished through a systems
approach to transformative change versus a piecemeal approach to
incremental improvement. By its nature, transformation cannot be
achieved through a project-by-project approach. Rather, it must be
carefully linked to a large-scale plan to drive system-wide changes designed to significantly impact student outcomes.

Ensuring the success of small projects is a routine part of management, but managing large-scale changes that significantly impact mission and goal-specific outcomes is the task of a transformation leader.
While managing small projects, leaders would do well to maintain their
focus at the system level because that is where the big pay-offs occur.

Prioritize Students

Up to this point, the focus of this chapter has largely been on transforming the business side of the enterprise, which tends to be more
sharply defined and more readily subject to consensus than change in
the academic enterprise. There is little doubt, however, that gainful
change in student learning outcomes is realized by transformation of
the academic core.

Imagine today's technology savvy student who can access information
at the speed of a search engine (and bandwidth capability) entering a
college where professors play the role of sage on the stage, testing for
rote memorization of facts and figures, and using the learning management system strictly as a repository for a course syllabus and extra read-
ings. Looking to the future, Nick Gidwani, the founder of SkilledUp,
sees "scant hope for 200 professors, all delivering the same lecture."[14]

or any educational leader who follows the blogs of Seth Godin, or for that matter, policy makers and pundits, it is widely believed that the industrial model of education in the United States has failed a large percentage of our population. In his blog post "The specter of the cult of ignorance" Godin states:

> The industrial school had several generations and billions of dollars to drill and practice us into game show champions, and it has failed, miserably. Cultural literacy is essential. A common store of knowledge is the only way to create community, to build and integrate a tribe of people interested in living together in harmony. But that store of knowledge will never be infinite, and what's more important, we cannot drill and practice it into a population that has so many fascinating or easy diversions available as alternatives.[15]

The information age has brought talent mismatches to every industry, and education is no exception. McKinsey and Company estimates, for example, that about half of the end-to-end processes in banks (e.g., opening an account or getting a car loan) can be fully automated. Automation is now prevalent across economic sectors, from manufacturing to bookkeeping to retail, and it is predicted that "47% of occupations could be automated in the next few decades."[16]

Even knowledge-intensive fields, such as oncology diagnostics, are susceptible to challenge by machines. Machine intelligence, like IBM's Watson, has the ability to scan and store massive amounts of medical research and magnetic resonance imaging (MRI) results and, therefore, is capable of diagnosing cancers with much higher levels of speed and accuracy than is possible by skilled physicians. Digitization will encroach on knowledge roles across industries.

The challenge for community colleges will be to balance automated services with traditional human resources to optimally drive student success. For example, technology can be used to alter instruction so that instructors can spend more time working individually with students, and students can spend more time engaging with the content and learning materials, enabling a focus on higher-level learning in contrast to rote memorization.

In addition to developing new programs to prepare the workers who will maintain automated systems, a key challenge for leaders will be the reallocation of savings from internal automation to the human talent needed to drive mission-specific outcomes.[17] Recent testing of hybrid or technology-enabled teaching formats at the college level (e.g., combining MOOC delivery with in-class instruction) revealed outcomes that are comparable to traditional teaching formats but with considerably reduced class time.[18]

Reports show that students in hybrid courses had the same or slightly better outcomes than traditionally taught students, as measured by pass rates, assessment scores, and grades. According to researchers Rebecca Griffiths, Matthew Chingos, Christine Mulhern, and Richard Spies, "Our findings add empirical weight to an emerging consensus that technology can be used to enhance productivity in higher education by reducing costs without compromising student outcomes."[19]

The economies of scale realized through open education resources (OER) serve not only to lower the price of learning and expand access to knowledge and skills needed for employment, but also to improve individual student learning outcomes. With globalization and automation as the norm, demand for retraining and continuing education will soar among workers of all ages.

As content that enables customization and purpose-driven education expands in an increasingly accessible online environment, community college leaders, particularly those who have ridden the disruptive wave by building robust online delivery systems, will have a distinct advantage over the Ivies that created MOOCs and those lesser-known institutions that have followed suit without fanfare. Why? Given their already low-cost structures and unparalleled agility as a sector of higher education, community colleges that tap the right talent to curate the best content from the likes of MIT and Harvard, and then effectively deliver a customized and purposeful learning experience via online platforms, will have a distinct advantage in the marketplace both today and in the foreseeable future because of their extraordinary value proposition.

Maintain Constancy of Purpose over the Transformation Journey

It takes time to transform an organization, and if the current turnover rates among community college CEOs holds or worsens, it is likely that the transformation agenda will be enacted over the tenure of more than one CEO. Constancy of purpose must be maintained over time, and the transformation agenda must become deeply engrained in the culture and organizational systems so that it will be difficult for a new CEO to undo it. The period of transition presents a potential problem given that change agendas for performance improvement far too often become associated with a particular CEO as opposed to an institutional mandate owned by every stakeholder, especially the governing board.

Given that boards are at the top of the authority chain in the organization, transformation requires more than passive support from this governing entity. "Boards do, and must, have a powerful role in establishing institutional 'will' for improvement . . . this will require that the Board demonstrate backbone, and send a clear set of signals to the organization that [the college] will achieve [its] quality aims, even if the required changes are painful."[20] By prioritizing and closely monitoring progress along key performance metrics, holding executives accountable for achieving target goals, allocating resources in support of the transformation agenda, establishing policies to drive quality improvement, and acting steadfastly and courageously in response to predictable challenges, governing boards will ensure constancy of purpose over the transformational journey.

PATHWAYS TO TRANSFORMATION

Transformation is a journey, and there are many ways to get there. Reinertsen[21] describes the following pathways to transformation as common among organizations:

- Revolution: grassroots leadership
- Friendly takeover: leadership from outside
- Intentional macrosystem transformation: leadership from *high* above
- Intentional organizational transformation: leadership from above

Whatever pathway is ultimately traveled, it bears repeating that transformation takes time. Once an organization is transformed, its embedded DNA has changed so much that it is largely unrecognizable from its

previous state. Sustained energy is required to achieve this level of transformation, and it is not just leadership energy. Organizational energy—
collective motivation, enthusiasm, and intense commitment—is a crucial
ingredient of successful transformation.

Revolution

There is little doubt that a critical factor in the transformation of
community colleges will be a change in the culture of the professional
workforce. A shift will occur from individual faculty autonomy and professional hierarchies to a team approach, and from disengagement from
college goals to "college citizenship." Consider, for example, a scenario
in which a new generation of faculty revolt against the old system. This
would be a powerful incentive for dramatic change and hence constitute a revolution. As opportunities arise, leaders can selectively support
grassroots leadership or "revolution" and accelerate cultural change.

Friendly Takeover

A transition currently underway is the shift of power from the college
and its faculty to students and their families who increasingly have the
power of information in making the choices consistent with their needs.
As competition heats up, this shift in power will drive a broad range of
changes, including radical redesign of how education is delivered, paid
for, measured, and reported.

Ultimately, the power shift to students and families will result in
greater influence on where resources are invested. As with revolution,
leadership exerted from outside, or friendly takeover of the educational
experience by students and their families, can be reinforced by leaders
to expedite change.

Intentional Macrosystem Transformation

The intentional acts of policy makers, regulators, and others in positions of influence and authority represent another pathway to transformation. Transformation can be accelerated by, and sometimes is
dependent upon, macrosystem changes. A 2014 Jobs for the Future

report titled *Policy Meets Pathways: A State Policy Agenda for Transformational Change*[22] called for sweeping changes that would affect all students, not just the few participating in pilot programs on individual campuses. Seven policy actions were recommended for states to increase graduation rates:

- Streamline academic requirements and create clearly structured programs of study
- Accelerate students through developmental education
- Expand student-support services, including early alerts and advising interventions when students go off course
- Ensure that structured pathways lead to credentials and competencies that help students get jobs with family-sustaining wages
- Use statewide data systems to track students through college and into the labor market.
- Receive financial incentives to improve persistence and completion rates.
- Expand faculty-led professional-development activities to improve teaching and learning

Macrosystem changes are difficult to disregard as a basis for transformation. They shape institutional systems and processes and ultimately funding streams. They are the equivalent of riding the jet stream for leaders seeking a fast track to transformation.[23]

Intentional Organizational Transformation

Intentional organizational transformation is a carefully planned and executed approach to transformation using the full resources of an institution. This approach is preferable for colleges and universities because it unfolds in stages and enables personnel to adjust gradually to change. Most often it takes the form of initiatives from visionary leaders who place a change agenda at the leading edge, rather than the trailing edge, of transformation. However, no matter how carefully considered this pathway to transformation might be, it would be an error for leaders to assume that they can bring about transformation without convergence with other pathways.[24]

The transformation journey is arduous and complex, and it is not unreasonable to assume that help from enabling agents inside and outside the college may be required to complete the journey.

LEADERSHIP MODEL FOR TRANSFORMATION

As we have stated throughout this book, leaders broadly distributed throughout an organization sharing a common language and conversant with change have the best chance of success in leading transformation. These dispersed leaders, however, rarely undertake transformation solely on the basis of intuition and instinct. A model of some kind is required and it should be customized to the unique circumstances and characteristics of the institution and its most prominent leaders—the executive team and board. Whatever the model, once selected, it becomes an essential tool for leading the transformation process, and it should be widely understood and deployed.

Any transformation leadership model assumes a complex and dynamic organization. Therefore, a framework for navigating the process is more of a guide than a set of rigid directions to a destination. The destination can gain dimension and clarity further down the pathway as it comes into focus; it does not have to be crystal clear at the beginning of the journey. What follows is a description of fundamental leadership actions essential for community college practitioners leading transformation. These actions rely heavily on Kotter's[25] change model that remains a definitive cross-industry guide for leading transformation.

Transformation is a change process that moves through a series of phases, each of which require considerable time and attention. "Skipping steps may create the illusion of speed, but rarely produces a satisfying result."[26] According to Kotter, "critical mistakes in any of the phases can have a devastating impact, slowing momentum and negating hard-won gains. Perhaps because leaders have limited experience in transforming or reinventing organizations, even capable individuals make at least one big error."[27] The error, however, should not be one of failure to adopt a proven change model that includes, at a minimum, the following elements:

1. Communicate the urgency
2. Create and communicate a compelling future-state

3. Empower others to move the change forward
4. Remove obstacles
5. Create a change coalition
6. Create short-term wins
7. Build on the change
8. Anchor change in the culture

Communicate the Urgency

"CEOs who give lip service to transformation will find others doing the same. Only the boss . . . can ensure that the right people spend the right amount of time driving the necessary changes."[28] Communicating a sense of urgency about the need for change, particularly change that is intended to transform the organization, can spark the initial motivation to launch a transformation agenda.

Momentum building is not simply a matter of sharing negative enrollment or ranting about increased competition. Rather, an open and convincing dialogue about the condition of the higher education industry and the strategies competitors are using to increase market share can engage stakeholders in meaningful conversation about the cost of doing nothing, and the urgency can build and feed on itself.

Kotter[29] suggests that for change to be successful, 75 percent of the team must buy into the change; for this to happen significant time and energy on front-end work, which includes identifying and engaging a network of leaders both within and beyond the organization, is a must.

Transformation leaders should be transparent about the transformation agenda and performance measures, particularly areas of underperformance that are putting the organization at risk. Some performance goals are self-evident (e.g., improved job placement of graduates) and do not need a business case. Other goals, however, do need explanation. For example, making a clear linkage between improvement in enrollment processes and financial results may be necessary to motivate employees who are "process owners," that is, individuals directly involved in the tedious work of managing a process who may mightily resist change because they "own" and attribute inherent value to the way things have always been done.

For a new president, transparency about performance measures may be construed as criticism or even an indictment of the previous administration. As a new president, one of the authors entering an environment that had become financially upside down (65 percent of resources allocated to administrative overhead) had to quickly assess and communicate to stakeholders the reality of the college's financial condition. Critically important was putting a face on the bad news delivered to stakeholders through student stories and data sharing, and launching a strategic planning process in which questions regarding why immediate budget adjustments were necessary were easily and honestly answerable. Transparency also helped the governing board to get behind the transformation agenda set forth in the strategic plan that was carefully deliberated and unanimously approved.

For long-serving leaders, failure can result from underestimating the risk involved in complacency or the inability to break out of complacency. Kotter estimates that 50 percent of organizations fail in this phase of transformation, in part because leaders tend to underestimate the challenge of shaking people out of their comfort zones.[30] Sometimes leaders lack the patience for transformation work, or on the flip side, they become paralyzed by downside possibilities that could leave them in the untenable position of being blamed for creating a crisis.

A paralyzed senior management often comes from having too many managers and not enough leaders. Management's mandate is to minimize risk and to keep the current system operating. Change, by definition, requires creating a new system, which in turn always demands leadership. Phase one in a renewal process typically goes nowhere until enough real leaders are promoted or hired into senior-level jobs.[31]

Leaders may be deemed to act inappropriately when airing an institution's dirty laundry (i.e., financial underperformance). A tough lesson many leaders have learned in explaining budgetary performance is that poor financial performance, although effective as a means of motivating change, can be both a blessing and a curse in the early phase of transformation. Losing money catches people's attention, but it also leaves fewer resources for maneuvering and managing change.

Create and Communicate a Compelling Future-State

Transformation requires enormous energy. As discussed previously, linking concepts and ideas to a carefully crafted vision that can be easily grasped and remembered helps employees to understand why they are being asked to do something different than what they have always done. Once a transformation agenda is launched, faculty and staff are being asked to rethink and reshape the organization while continuing day-to-day operations.

This is asking a lot and it will meet with resistance unless individuals can actually envision and personalize a future-state on their own terms. The leader's transformation story must, at minimum, answer: "Why are we changing?" "How will we get there?" and "How will this affect me?" Concerns and anxieties should be addressed openly and honestly.

A leader must declare a compelling future-state personally, publicly, repeatedly, and irrevocably. When leaders are able to personalize the story with powerful individual experiences and anecdotes to underline their determination and belief—and to demonstrate that obstacles can be overcome—the transformation story gains energy. When the story is clear and memorable, employees can more readily embrace transformation and begin to infuse it with their own personal meaning.

Consider the experience of one of our authors whose change initiative was expedited by financial exigency. She sought to show how the college's lopsided resource allocation model was actually depriving students of the advising and support services needed to achieve their educational and career goals. Using real student stories that were clearly supported by Community College Survey of Student Engagement (CCSSE), Integrated Postsecondary Education Data System (IPEDS), and other available data, her message consistently connected the dots between improved financials and student success.

Once the story of a compelling future-state is crafted, the leader's role is one of constant reinforcement. The "vision speech" must be delivered often—both formally and informally—and across multiple audiences, with the goal of enabling change leaders throughout the organization and beyond its walls to describe the vision on demand in five minutes or less. Talking about it at every opportunity and keeping the vision central to daily operations and problem solving keeps it fresh on everyone's mind. Reinforcement occurs through incorporation of the vision into all aspects of operations, from onboarding new employees to performance reviews.

It is important to "walk the talk." What one does is far more important—and believable—than what one says. By regularly meeting with students and staff and conveying the necessity of a business model centered on student success, leaders demonstrate the kind of behavior they want from others. Ultimately employees weigh the actions of their leaders, from the president to the dean to the faculty senate leader, to determine whether they believe in the vision of what the future could be.

Empower Others

We know that leaders alone cannot induce change. It is the power of a group moving in the same direction that really gets things moving. People resist change and take comfort in the status quo even when the institution is experiencing difficulty. It is important, therefore, to mobilize others not only through a compelling vision of what is possible, but also through the efforts of thought leaders who hold sway over faculty and staff.

Kotter[32] argues that by empowering people in the institution, leaders create a "volunteer army." "The volunteer army is not a bunch of grunts carrying out orders from the brass. Its members are change leaders who bring energy, commitment, and enthusiasm."[33] It is this type of grassroots leadership and network in community colleges that gets the work of transformation done. Transformation requires a cadre of leaders who are capable of motivating others and tapping leadership potential throughout the institution.

The power of building and tapping into leadership potential throughout the institution was demonstrated by one of our authors during a transformational leadership experience. An experienced strategic leader (formerly chief of staff for an army general) was hired as the chief human resource officer. This was a critical early step for ensuring that every aspect of performance management was reviewed and fully aligned with the strategic plan and transformation agenda.

Once the organizational restructuring necessary to advance change was complete, the new human resources chief worked closely with the president to prepare new position descriptions aligned with strategic goals and to painstakingly manage the search process for each new hire. The goal was to hire change agents to act as leaders distributed throughout the college—the volunteer army. At the same time, the human resource officer was involved in the identification of internal high potential (HI-PO) employees for targeted professional development in change management.

In addition, the human resources leader updated the performance review instruments and process for administrators, faculty, and staff; on the other end of the human resources spectrum, he managed the intricacies of sundry types of employment separations that were necessary to clear the way for investment in the human resources needed to drive organizational transformation.

Remove Obstacles

Success in leading a change agenda requires a relentless focus on results, at system, process, and organizational levels. Measurable results toward the end goal must become a management responsibility that is routinely monitored across functional areas as part of a robust institutional effectiveness infrastructure. Through conscious, planned effort, everyone in the organization should have clarity about his or her role in achieving the transformation agenda.

Ideally, as part of a comprehensive evaluation process, each individual would clearly articulate his or her work in advancing the transformation agenda. "The process of engaging each individual starts with the CEO, and is 'cascaded' throughout the organization in hundreds of conversations between managers and their direct reports."[34] Communicating the shared vision helps to illuminate both opportunities and barriers to achieving transformation objectives.

Pockets of resistance and business-as-usual processes and structures getting in the way of change are barriers to achieving a desired state. Transformation leaders must firmly put in place an infrastructure for change and continually monitor for barriers and obstacles. Removing obstacles empowers employees to execute the vision and is a key step in moving change forward.

Helpful in this regard is a process of "mapping team members on a matrix, with 'business performance' on one axis and 'role-modeling desired behavior' on the other. Those in the top-right box (desired behavior, high performance) are the organization's stars, and those in the bottom-left box (undesired behavior, low performance) should be motivated, developed, or dismissed."[35]

During this phase, leaders should:

- Identify and develop internal talent, or hire key leaders whose main roles are to deliver the change.
- Review organizational structure, job descriptions, and performance and compensation systems to ensure alignment with the vision.
- Recognize and reward people for making change happen.
- Identify people who are resisting change, and help them to understand expectations.
- Take action to remove barriers (human or otherwise).

Removing barriers can occur in a number of ways. One way is to alter the mental maps of employees who create barriers to change.[36] Another tactic is to use expert talent management, which can provide a critical resource for driving systems and organizational results and removing obstacles.

Create a Change Coalition

Successful transformation requires strong and visible support from employees in every part of the organization. Getting the right people leading the initiative is essential, but even with the right people in place, "it takes time for a group of intelligent, ambitious, and committed people to align themselves in a clear direction."[37]

Typically, the first order of business is for members to agree on what they can achieve as a team (not as individuals), how often the team should meet, what transformation issues should be discussed, and what behavior the team expects (and will not tolerate). These agreements are often summarized in a "team charter" for leading the transformation, and the CEO can periodically use the charter to ensure that the team is on the right track.[38]

Given the importance of teambuilding, one of the authors brought together individuals with diverse backgrounds and industries—from higher education to corporations to nonprofits—to tackle a transformation challenge. She convened the team periodically in a casual setting as part of a twelve-person book club to stimulate dialogue about managing change and to assess team capacity.

The books selected focused on managing change, so the relevance to each member of the team was immediate, and the dialogue robust.

Relationship building between and among individuals was perhaps the greatest benefit of the book club meetings. There was significant value in reviewing progress toward goals and making on-the-spot adjustments in tactics to align the work of the team. Far more valuable was the opportunity to talk together in a nonthreatening environment about theories of change versus what people were actually experiencing on the ground, which provided an extraordinary learning opportunity and camaraderie.

By letting down their guard and sharing personal stories of everyday victories and failures, the group learned from each other and there was a poignant realization that everyone was engaged in the same painstaking, exhausting, and exhilarating experience of managing change. The team meetings were, of course, supplemental to more formal progress meetings at which each leader reported performance metrics relative to plan.

Bringing a team together regularly to share results and to keep the transformation initiatives, budgets, and financial targets on track is a tedious but necessary part of managing a change coalition. As a rule of thumb, 80 percent of the team's time should be devoted to dialogue, with 20 percent invested in presentations. Effective dialogue requires a well-structured agenda to ensure that ample time is "spent in personal reflection (to ensure that each person forms an independent point of view from the outset), discussion in small groups (refining the thinking and exploring second- and third-level assumptions), and discussion by the full team before final decisions are made."[39]

In addition to the senior team, effective change leaders can and must be identified throughout the organization; they do not necessarily reside only at the top of the hierarchy. In fact, the hierarchical structure may be the first thing to go. Leading change requires a coalition of influential people whose power comes from a variety of sources, including job title, status, expertise, and political influence. Once formed, the "change coalition" must work as a team, continuing to build urgency and momentum around the need for change.[40]

Create Short-Term Wins

Nothing motivates more than success. A powerful way to reinforce the end goal is to spotlight success along the way. Sharing success stories "helps crystallize the meaning of transformation and gives people confidence that it will actually work."[41] Focusing on what went wrong can generate feelings of fatigue, blame, and resistance, whereas high-lighting what worked can foster creativity and the desire to succeed. Providing stakeholders with a taste of victory throughout the change process by spotlighting wins can also neutralize naysayers and negative thinkers.

Consider the tactic employed by one of the authors who required senior managers to produce monthly communiqués in which they high-lighted progress toward key goals for all employees and key stakehold-ers. The transparency went a long way toward creating an open environment in which every member of the campus community was regularly reminded of the vision and steps in that direction, and they had the opportunity to respond with ideas, insights, or suggestions.

Receiving broad-based feedback from faculty and staff, and the mere act of chronicling progress, was energizing to the leader, and when positive feedback was received from stakeholders, it reinforced the importance of the work for everyone involved. Transformation does not take one masterstroke. Creating short-term targets leading to a long-term goal makes the end seem more achievable. The change team may have to work hard to come up with achievable targets, but each "win" can further motivate staff.[42]

Specific, achievable improvement projects are key leverage points—highly visible moments—in the transformation process. Discrete projects with stretch goals for improvement, capable leadership, and organizational support can yield easily observed results and deliver the added benefit of demonstrating the values and behaviors that drive successful transformation. Channeling attention to positive change can build commitment to the change initiative by providing staff with touchstones that connect the present state of the organization with a desired future-state.

To create short-term wins, leaders should:

- Look for "low hanging fruit," which are projects that can be implemented without assistance from strong critics of the change.
- Choose early targets that are inexpensive as a means of justifying investment in a project.
- Analyze the pros and cons of established targets; failure to succeed with an early goal can imperil the entire change initiative.
- Reward people who are champions in meeting targets.

Build on the Change

Real change runs deep, and Kotter argues that many change projects fail because victory is declared too early.[43] Quick wins are only the beginning of what needs to be accomplished to achieve long-term change. Transformation leaders need to perpetually be on the lookout for improvements. Each success provides an opportunity to build on what went right and to identify what can be improved. Also, ideas remain fresh when new change agents and leaders are added to the change coalition.[44]

"Transformation requires depth and breadth of improvement, which cannot be achieved without innovations and designs that depart from convention."[45] This level of change is difficult to achieve in the absence of activities designed to expose the organization to a wide range of ideas and to encourage innovation. Such activities might include identifying "beacons" or best performers in a given area of operations. The CEO might make a habit of asking "What is the highest level of performance a college could achieve in this area (e.g., student retention)?" "Have you studied the research and findings?" "What did you learn?"

Continuously seeking new ideas—both from outside and from within—and developing a fast-track capability to test new ideas and report out the results contributes to a culture of inquiry and innovation. Trying out new ideas reinforces the inherent value of ideation and creativity, which becomes self-perpetuating. Although not every idea can be tested, and staff whose ideas are not tested may become discouraged, it is safe to say that neither idea generation nor testing of ideas has reached a level of activity in higher education that would pose a threat to capacity. In other words, the upside of continuous ideation and testing is in the change-adept culture that emerges from the practice.

Anchor Change in the Culture

Rooting improvements made along the transformation journey into organizational culture is a continuous challenge. To bring enduring change to habits of thought and behavior, these desired habits must become part of the core of the organization. Anchoring change in culture takes time and must be approached with intentionality and resolve.

Some lessons are learned the hard way. For one of the authors and her leadership team, efforts at structuring campus presentations and communications around the big goal of 100 percent student success were met with unexpected skepticism. There was considerable resistance from faculty in the beginning—grounded in the poor-students-equal-poor-results argument—but over time and through persistence, faculty began to base their research proposals and instructional initiatives on the big goal, thereby anchoring the goal in academic culture. The takeaway was that leaders must consistently and persistently connect the dots between organizational change and student success to foster lasting cultural change.

Intentional action to achieve change in the faculty culture must be thoughtfully planned and as close to flawlessly executed as possible. The calcified faculty-centric culture and deep attachment to individual autonomy is a formidable barrier to the consistent, reliable use of evidence in measuring student learning outcomes.

Methods for using faculty autonomy and channeling it into positive energy must be customized to the cultural features of each college. Creating opportunities for faculty to work in cross-disciplinary teams that focus on the needs of individual students or student cohorts, perhaps using a case-management approach, has the potential to personalize the work and highlight the upside of change.

Engaging students more frequently and more fully in improvement efforts can reinforce the responsibility that instructors and staff bear for student success. Anchoring change in faculty culture is, without a doubt, a significant challenge for transformation leaders across the college, even those within the faculty ranks. It will tax the resolve of the most patient and accepting of leaders, but what is the alternative? The simple answer is that there is no alternative; leaders must do what it takes to see change through to a successful conclusion.

To invigorate the change process over the long term and refresh staff commitment, leaders should:

- Talk about progress at every opportunity. Tell success stories about the change process, and describe the experience of staff who are part of the process.

- Emphasize change ideals and values when hiring and training new faculty and staff.
- Publicly recognize members of the change coalition, and ensure that staff—new and old—remember their contributions.
- Create plans to replace key change leaders as they move on. Advance planning will ensure that their legacy is not lost or forgotten.

A key takeaway is that leading transformation requires the identification of leaders and the development of skill sets that differ quite strikingly from those needed in the past.

TRADITIONAL MODE LEADERS

What are traditional mode leaders? What intrinsic traits and personal values do they have that distinguish them as leaders? Most community college leaders arrive at executive-level positions via progressive movement from faculty roles into higher levels of administration. It is not unusual for successful executives to be entrenched in the that-is-the-way-it-is-done approach to management.[46] When all indicators would seem to suggest that past ways of doing things have yielded success, why change?

A cursory glance at advertisements for community college presidents reveals that the hiring process for leaders remains static. In a somewhat sardonic editorial, Milton Greenberg[47] points to the tired list of desired traits in advertisements for almost every senior-level administrative job in higher education. These typically include:

- The ability to articulate a vision
- A collaborative working style
- The capacity to lead and inspire diverse groups
- A commitment to excellence
- Superb communication skills
- Distinguished scholarly and professional achievement
- Well-developed interpersonal skills
- An ability to work effectively with a wide range of constituents
- A commitment to diversity

The standard set of talents and skills required for leadership positions ranging from deans to presidents are often gleaned from an institutional needs analysis that involves a wide range of stakeholders, which would suggest that despite obvious differences in the size and reputation of American colleges and universities, "missions are widely shared, or else we could not claim a higher-education societal purpose."[48]

When it comes to search processes and the quiescent involvement of governing boards, search committees, and others with legitimate roles in the hiring process, community colleges are no different than their higher education counterparts in using a three-dimensional printer approach to creating and selecting leaders. A harsh view of this approach would liken it to a process of cloning in which stereotypical leaders are developed by curmudgeonly gatekeepers who control access to the executive office. Input the standard list of requirements, mix thoroughly, and a leader will emerge who is likely ill-prepared for the challenge of leading a college in a tumultuous landscape.

Pundits are quick to opine that "higher education has lost its status as a revered enterprise and is now grounded with self-serving industries of which buyers should be wary."[49] And there is growing sentiment that the next generation of leaders should be prepared to take a wrecking ball to the standard model where "professionals . . . untrained in teaching, and unaccountable for student learning—dominate every aspect of higher education . . . and students are cheated by this structural inattention to their academic well-being."[50]

This is a stunningly narrow view of leadership in modern-day colleges, but its existence is telling of what will be expected of the next generation of leaders. They will need, in addition to a commitment to excellence, the risk-tolerance, grit, and tenacity required for demolition and the structural rebuilding of their colleges. This will be perhaps the most daunting challenge facing leaders who are intent on the industry transformation that is long overdue.

CHARACTERISTICS OF TRANSFORMATIONAL LEADERS

In view of the complex set of challenges involved in leading and managing organizational transformation, advertisements for future generation leaders will look different from what is in print today. Published requisites might include:

- Understands the fundamentals of change management
- Possesses demonstrated experience in applying technology solutions for resource optimization
- Possesses a track record of using business intelligence to drive organizational performance, operational efficiency, and agility
- Demonstrates a capacity to use open education resources and artificial intelligence to improve student learning productivity
- Ability to orchestrate distributed leadership and leverage talent within and outside the organization to achieve mission and goals
- Uses technology solutions to enhance teaching, learning, and student support

Leaders of the future must be "intrapreneurial," that is, they must be able to see alternative options for delivering results, many of which will involve risk. At the same time, intrapreneurial leaders must be able to forecast, model, and apply solutions that yield ever-higher returns on institutional investment in student success.

Intrapreneurial

In addition to understanding and being able to apply the fundamentals of change management and possessing demonstrated experience in the use of technology to drive value for students, leaders will need to be adept at lateral thinking. Lateral thinking "is concerned not with playing with the existing pieces, but with seeking to change those very pieces."[51]

In the same way that sixteen-year-old Dick Fosbury changed the rules of the high jump and won an Olympic gold medal in the 1960s by abandoning the "straddle" technique (running straight and clearing the bar face-down) in favor of what is now known as the "Fosbury flop" (running diagonally and jumping over the bar backward), effective leaders will need to rethink assumptions about the organization and operations, in essence creating "a new game for competitors to catch up to."[52]

Figuring out how to encourage unconventional thinking throughout the organization, the kind of thinking that leads to breakthroughs, while managing inherent risk will be a base-level requirement for new leaders.

Because most organizations, particularly hierarchical organizations such as community colleges, are not set up to encourage rule-bending—and given the realities of a highly regulated industry—leaders will be required to employ dual-system thinking to successfully manage both compliance and the development of intrapreneurs.

Intrapreneurs are lateral thinkers who are able to distinguish between the accepted or "right" approach and the new and perhaps "best" approach for achieving a desired outcome. Intrapreneurs are good candidates for the dual systems required in today's change environment.[53] Intrapreneurs succeed where others fail by asking the following questions:

- What are the assumptions inherent to the question?
- How could we change the question?
- What if we could not take the conventional approach?
- What if we had to do this 100 times cheaper?
- What if we had to do this 10 times over?[54]

Risk Tolerant

Closely related to creating lateral thinking in the institution is the ability of leaders to create a high tolerance for risk and a passion for innovation. Although somewhat counterintuitive, the old-fashioned workplace walkabout may be a necessary habit for new leaders in an effort to avoid roadblocks to innovation.

The walkabout generates opportunities for leaders to listen to employees and students, which in turn produces opportunities to gain insights from the front line. These interactions build trust and ultimately create the cultural competency and agility to compete in a dynamic market.[55] "Risk that fuels achievement can only really be encouraged in cultures that are deeply trusting and deeply grounded in win/win thinking."[56] Top to bottom, the ways in which individuals and organizations perceive and operate inside risk are intertwined with values grounded in trust and continuous learning.

An understanding and appreciation of organizational learning will be critical for the next generation of leaders, as will an openness to risk and the failures that may accompany it. For organizational and individual learning to occur, however, leaders must be able to create opportunities that allow for productive failure.[57] The extent to which leaders embrace risk and the manner in which they handle it will be an important barometer of an institution's capacity for transformation.

Adept at Managing Inherent Capability

Using a business model reliant on a large adjunct workforce loosely connected to the institution to deliver instruction to increasingly larger classes may work in the short term, but next-generation leaders will need to be more innovative with instructional strategy and design. Leaders who are managing through transformation today and those who will follow them will grapple with three primary tensions: price versus value (specifically with regard to diminishing returns), access orientation versus a success orientation, and high-touch versus high-tech instruction.

Complacent leaders—particularly administrators and boards—will either be undone by the steady erosion brought about by obsolete financial models or "caught in a vortex of shifting collective consciousness" as waves of industry transformation proceed,[58] whereas successful leaders will determine how to gain advantage by finding opportunity in the competing sides of each tension.

For price versus value, the primary criterion for decision making may be return on investment. When establishing tuition levels and operating budgets, if decisions are measured in accord with delivering the most value to the most students, then making decisions about expenses that are peripheral to the core mission become somewhat easier.

Think about the following exchange between a community college president and the headmaster of a highly ranked private high school in the Northeast. A question posed to the headmaster concerned how he could possibly compete with peer institutions while operating out of cinder-block buildings with austere interiors. He revealed that his competitive advantage lay in small class sizes and highly qualified teachers who considered student learning to be the top priority, which resulted in a high percentage of graduates moving on to highly ranked colleges and universities.

The elusive formula for success can actually be pretty simple: educate and graduate students who succeed in achieving their goals. Favorable education outcomes are certainly a priority for community college students, and they expect to receive an education that leads to competitiveness when it comes to university transfer or job attainment. Thus, the ability to effectively manage the price-value tension is critical.

The tension between access and success is evident as input measures are pitted with outcomes. Instead of falling prey to the tyranny of either–or, community college leaders must reconcile competing aims and retain both an access orientation *and* a success orientation, but this is tricky territory and must be carefully managed. Managing with an eye to the linkage between these aims will involve intensive data collection and analysis that provides precise information needed to establish admission policies, placement guidelines, and course and program learning objectives that enable institutions to optimize access and success.

Once again, old models will not work as funding tightens, demands for accountability ramp up, and comparative data are readily available (e.g., College Scorecard) to assist students in making enrollment decisions on the basis of institutional performance. With more states moving to performance-based funding, it is important to focus on specific outcome measures of student success, but at the same time factor in their impact on access. Community colleges need both access *and* student success.

A final tension playing out in higher education institutions today involves the high-touch culture of community colleges in which faculty and staff perform a nurturing role with students versus the influx of high-tech curricula and instruction that alter human interaction. Like aims of access and success that are pitted as contradictory, the trade-offs between high touch and high tech do not necessarily occur to the detriment of students.

Engagement with students clearly results in positive outcomes relative to retention, graduation, and transfer, but engagement can occur in a variety of formats. Well-crafted online courses can include synchronous face time through video streaming, forums for robust discussion, and myriad opportunities for connecting students with instructors, other students, and the expanding world of online education resources.[59]

However, online courses will most likely not be sufficient to deliver the desired learning outcomes and student success rates in and of themselves. For example, research shows that students from poor academic backgrounds or those requiring developmental work do not fare well in an online environment.[60] Part of the challenge for change leaders is to determine ways to optimize the outcomes of high-tech instruction so that more students achieve success.

SUMMING UP

Time and place could not be better for transformation. Impending retirements and leadership transitions will provide ample opportunity for organizational transformation as 45 percent of sitting presidents are currently older than age 61, and 75 percent of sitting presidents are planning to retire within the next ten years.[61] Further, there is evidence of increasing reluctance on the part of "insiders"—vice presidents and deans—to aspire to or position themselves for the top job.

Once widely considered to be vaunted positions that bestowed upon the holder a certain status and "mystique," community college presidents currently evidence a high turnover rate, and votes of no confidence are so frequent as to be mundane. Relentless challenges associated with declining enrollment and austere budgets, underperformance on key metrics of student success, and the sclerotic culture of academe will likely increase the appeal of retirement or other forms of transition out of senior management roles.

The changing of the guard of senior administrators, whether through retirement, displacement, or the pursuit of new opportunities, provides space to rethink what it means to lead colleges at a time when all but the broad contours of the future are largely unknown. And it begs the question of how to prepare those who aspire to lead these institutions—institutions that are unsustainable left unchanged and, as a result, engaged in transformation either by design or default.

NOTES

1. Andrew Dyer, Grant Freeland, Steve Gunby, and Cynthia DeTar, "Leading Transformation: Conversations with Leaders on Driving Change," The Boston Consulting Group, October 2011, 4, http://www.bcg.com/documents/file87317.pdf.

2. Jeffrey J. Selingo, *The Innovative University: What College Presidents Think about Change in American Education* (Washington, DC: Chronicle of Higher Education, 2014).

3. James L. Reinertsen, "A Theory of Leadership for the Transformation for Health Care Organizations" (monograph, 2004), http://www.uft-a.com/PDF/Transformation.PDF.

4. Kotter, *Accelerate*.

5. Clayton Christen, "Disruptive Innovation and Catalytic Change," *Futures Forum*, Harvard Business School (2008): 44.

6. Stephen Covey, *The 7 Habits of Highly Effective People* (New York: Simon & Schuster, 2004).

7. Reinertsen, "A Theory of Leadership," 3.

8. Carolyn B. Aiken and Scott P. Keller, *The CEO's Role in Leading Transformation*, ¶ 4, http://www.mckinsey.com/insights/organization/the_ceos_role_in_leading_transformation

9. John P. Kotter and Dan S. Cohen, *The Heart of Change: Real-Life Stories of How People Change their Organizations* (Boston: Harvard Business Press, 2002).

10. Reinertsen, "A Theory of Leadership," 12.

11. Schumpeter, "Little Things That Mean a Lot," *The Economist* (blog), July 19, 2014, ¶ 8, http://www.economist.com/news/business/21607816-businesses-should-aim-lots-small-wins-big-data-add-up-something-big-little.

12. "Zimpher: More Than $6 Million Redirected to Students in First Year of Shared Services Initiative," *SUNY News,* September 19, 2012, http://www.suny.edu/suny-news/press-releases/september-2012/9-19-12-shared-services-savings/.

13. Colleen Flaherty, "Outsourced in Michigan," *Inside Higher Education*, July 21, 2014, ¶ 3, https://www.insidehighered.com/news/2014/07/21/colleges-assign-adjunct-hiring-third-party.

14. "The Digital Degree," *The Economist*, June 28, 2014, ¶ 14, http://www.economist.com/news/briefing/21605899-staid-higher-education-business-about-experience-welcome-earthquake-digital.

15. Seth Godin, "Stop Stealing Dreams: (What is School for?)" (2012), 49, http://sethgodin.typepad.com/files/stop-stealing-dreams6print.pdf.

16. "The Digital Degree." ¶ 10.

17. Martin Hirt and Paul Wilmott, "Strategic Principles for Competing in the Digital Age," *McKinsey Quarterly* (May 22, 2014), http://www.mckinsey.com/insights/strategy/strategic_principles_for_competing_in_the_digital_age.

18. Rebecca Griffiths, Matthew Chingos, Christine Mulhern, and Richard Spies, "Interactive Online Learning on Campus Testing: Testing MOOCs and Other Platforms in Hybrid Formats in the University of Maryland," ITHAKA,

July 10, 2014, http://sr.ithaka.org/research-publications/Interactive_Online_Learning_on_Campus_20140716.pdf.

19. Griffiths et al., "Interactive Online Learning," 4.

20. Reinertsen. "A Theory of Leadership," 12.

21. Reinertsen. "A Theory of Leadership."

22. Laura K. Couturier, *Policy Meets Pathways: A State Policy Agenda for Transformational Change* (Washington, DC: Jobs for the Future. 2014), 19, http://www.jff.org/sites/default/files/publications/materials/Policy-Meets-Pathways-121714.pdf.

23. Katherine Mangan, "A Call for Big Changes to Meet a Big Challenge at Community Colleges," *Chronicle of Higher Education*, December 18, 2014, http://chronicle.com/article/A-Call-for-Big-Changes-to-Meet/150927

24. Reinertsen, "A Theory of Leadership," 7.

25. Kotter, *Accelerate.*

26. John P. Kotter, "Why Transformational Efforts Fail," *Harvard Business Review* 73, no. 2 (1995): 59.

27. Kotter, "Why Transformational Efforts Fail," 60.

28. Aiken and Keller, *The CEO's Role*, ¶ 8.

29. Kotter, "Why Transformational Efforts Fail."

30. Kotter, "Why Transformational Efforts Fail."

31. Kotter, "Why Transformational Efforts Fail," 60.

32. John P. Kotter, "Accelerate!" *Harvard Business Review* (2012): 56.

33. Kotter, "Accelerate!" 56.

34. Reinertsen, "A Theory of Leadership," 15.

35. Aiken and Keller, *The CEO's Role*, ¶ 24.

36. J. Stewart Black and Hal B. Gregerson, *Leading Strategic Change: Breaking Through the Brain Barrier* (Upper Saddle River, NJ: Pearson Education, Inc., 2002).

37. Aiken and Keller, *The CEO's Role*, ¶ 32.

38. Aiken and Keller, *The CEO's Role*, ¶ 32.

39. Aiken and Keller, *The CEO's Role*, ¶ 34.

40. Kotter and Cohen, *The Heart of Change.*

41. Aiken and Keller, *The CEO's Role*, ¶ 15.

42. Kotter, "Accelerate!"

43. Kotter, *Accelerate.*

44. Kotter, "Accelerate!"

45. Reinertsen, "A Theory of Leadership," 14.

46. Shane Snow, "The Innovator's Question: What Would Fosbury Do?" *Harvard Business Review*, (September 8, 2014): ¶11, https://hbr.org/2014/09/the-innovators-question-what-would-fosbury-do/.

47. Milton Greenberg, "You Don't Need a Search Firm to Hire a President," *Chronicle of Higher Education*, September 1, 2014, http://chronicle.com/article/You-Dont-Need-a-Search-Firm/148525/.

48. Greenberg, "You Don't Need a Search Firm," ¶ 10.

49. Kevin Carey, "On the Immense Good Fortune of Higher Education," *Chronicle of Higher Education*, September 1, 2014, ¶ 7, http://chronicle.com/article/On-the-Immense-Good-Fortune-/148541/.

50. Carey, "On the Immense Good Fortune," ¶ 11.

51. Edward de Bono as cited in Snow, "The Innovator's Question," ¶ 7.

52. Snow, "The Innovator's Question," ¶ 8.

53. Kotter, *Accelerate*.

54. Snow, "The Innovator's Question."

55. Henry Doss, "Three Roadblocks to Innovation," *Forbes*, August 14, 2014, ¶ 12, http://www.forbes.com/sites/henrydoss/2014/08/14/there-are-three-roadblocks-to-innovation-do-a-walkabout-to-find-yours/.

56. Doss, "Three Roadblocks," ¶ 12.

57. Manu Kapur and Katharine Bielaczyc, "Designing for Productive Failure," *Journal of the Learning Sciences* 21, no.1 (2012): 45–83.

58. Carey, "On the Immense Good Fortune," ¶ 16.

59. Katrina A. Meyer, "Student Engagement Online: What Works and Why," *ASHE Higher Education Report*, 40, no. 6 (San Francisco: Jossey-Bass, 2014).

60. Shanna Smith Jaggars, Nikki Edgecombe, and Georgia West Stacey, "What we Know About Online Course Outcomes," (CCRC Teachers College Columbia University, New York, April, 2013), http://ccrc.tc.columbia.edu/media/k2/attachments/what-we-know-about-online-course-outcomes.pdf.

61. *The American College President 2012*.

4

DEVELOPING TOMORROW'S LEADERS

Today's technology-enabled, information-rich, deeply interconnected world means . . . we must begin to see schools, colleges and
classrooms as central points in larger networks of learning. If we
get this transformative technology revolution right, our generation
will literally enable the greatest expansion in access to high-quality
education opportunities in history.

—Arne Duncan[1]

It is clear that leaders are confronted by challenges that portend a different future for community colleges than the growth and expansion
that marked their early development. By their nature as colleges designed to meet the changing higher education needs of the communities
they serve, change has become part of every community college's DNA.

Now change along an incremental front is inadequate, and transformation is no longer an option; it is an imperative. Again, change is not
new to leaders and institutions; it has been part of their lexicon for years.
What is different today are its meaning and implications in a turbulent
landscape. No longer does change take the form of micro or incremental shifts (e.g., new technology and systems), which have a short-term
impact. Change now must be transformative and deep, enveloping the
entire institution and all in its employ.

New ways of thinking are necessary and more—much more—is required of leaders. The "more" is thinking deeply and differently about where community colleges are going and what must be done to get there. Leaders must be able to stretch the organization and leverage performance in ways that depart radically from current practice.[2] This puts a whole new spin on leadership, and it is the foundation upon which we frame a new way of thinking about leaders and leader development.

Crafting a new approach to leader development requires a decided break from how we have historically approached developing leaders. On-the-job training has been the primary vehicle for leader development.[3] Aspiring leaders watch and replicate what others do, they employ learned tactics in lower-level positions, and then they use these tactics and trial-and-error behaviors when leading from the top of the organization.

Leading during transformational change is different. Leaders must be able to read and calibrate the organizational context in which change is underway and move people and culture onto the same page regarding change—its pace and direction, its urgency, and its intensity. Learned tactics certainly have their place in navigating change, but they are not enough to successfully guide institutions through transformation.

Recognizing this, we begin by describing frame-breaking organizational practices that could be adopted by colleges and passed on to a new generation of leaders. We do this to illustrate the difference between convention and innovation in leadership practice. We avoid the trap of what could be done better by focusing on what must be done differently. Next, we explore existing approaches to leader development and highlight effective and ineffective practices. Finally, we offer recommendations on new and different approaches for preparing leaders for tomorrow's colleges.

LEADING FOR INNOVATION: FRAME-BREAKING PRACTICES

Community college leaders understand the importance of transformation and are taking steps to change their approach to management to fit the emerging landscape. The problem is that what is often described as change or "innovation"—internal leadership academies, job shadowing and mentoring, organizational restructuring, and the like—are often an extension of the current practice. Innovations of this type have an upside in that they expose mid-level and support staff to leadership dynamics that are part of strategic management. They also have a downside which, although well-intentioned, has much to do with the lack of innovation in leadership practice; *they lack imagination and reinforce the status quo.*

Recognizing that convention and innovation in leadership practice operate on a continuum that can easily blur distinctions between them, we provide the following examples of frame-breaking innovations in leadership practice that community colleges could adopt to improve leader effectiveness.

Reconceptualizing Leadership

What does it mean to be a leader? When we craft a different conception of leadership we do not picture merely putting new conductors on trains. Instead, we envision a fundamental shift in who we view as leaders, where we find them, and how we develop them. The basic hardwiring of leadership in community colleges needs to change, beginning with the breadth and location of positions in which the authority and power to lead resides. We now need new train tracks and new train stations.

Since the establishment of community colleges, talented individuals inside these institutions have been bypassed as potential leaders. Often this occurred because of explicit limitations (e.g., lack of access to stretch assignments, training programs, or capable mentors with transformational leadership skills). "More subtle, however, is the influence of what Linda Hill at Harvard University has labeled 'stylistic limitations'—attributes of personality that don't fit the conventional image of a leader."[4] Most often this happens when individuals are overlooked for top leadership positions because they do not exhibit the take-charge, direction-setting behavior we associate with leadership. In some instances it comes down to a cosmetic impression that "he or she does not look like a leader."

The size, complexity, and operating landscape of community colleges demand a more inclusive view of who can lead as well as greater breadth in the distribution of power. Leaders will be in abundant supply if we suspend unreasonable preconceptions of how they should look and act and broaden the base to include individuals of diverse background and skills who have the capacity for leadership. Examples might include individuals with a background in human resources or project management who can inspire and motivate a team; individuals with experience in community-based organizations who can bring grassroots organizing skills to management; individuals with experience in strategic planning who can chart a strategic direction; and individuals with a passion for innovation who can energize change.

When Google sought to determine what made for a great boss, topping the list was being a good coach and the capacity to empower a group.[5] The emphasis in Google's culture is on the end user—supporting employees so they can be at their best for the company's consumers. In all of this what is most important is recognition of the difference between convention (who has the *credentials to lead*) and intuition (who has the *potential to lead*).

Rethinking Power and Governance

Community college instructors and staff will look different tomorrow than we find them today. The multiple generations concurrently at work are changing the constructs of the job.[6] There are patterns of loyalty, needs for encouragement and support, and preferences for communication that separate older and younger workers. The nature of differentiation among workplace generations tends to be either overblown or seriously underestimated, but significant are its implications for the use and distribution of power in organizations, in particular, a growing tension between *old* and *new* power.[7]

The construct of old and new power and the analysis that follows build on the ideas of Heimans and Timms.[8] Old power is like currency. It is held by a few and once gained is guarded and carefully expended. "It is closed, inaccessible, and leader-driven. It downloads."[9] New power is different, working more like a current. It is open and participatory and created and used by many. "It uploads and distributes and is most forceful when it surges."[10] New power needs to be channeled, not guarded.

What does this have to do with leadership in community colleges? The balance between old and new power among workplace generations will become a defining issue for community colleges. If we view power as "the ability to produce intended effects,"[11] it follows that old and new power will produce effects differently. Old power requires follower behavior—individuals carrying out decisions, adhering to customs, and following rules. New power taps into individuals' capacity for growth and their desire to participate in organizational strategic actions—identifying opportunities, problem solving, and helping to chart a future direction—all occurring without being told.

This new look at power is a reflection of the way youth think and act in contemporary American culture. Infused in their lives is a preference for participatory behavior such as self-created content on Facebook, Twitter, and Instagram. A teen with her own YouTube channel engages with others as a content creator rather than as a passive recipient of someone else's ideas. Today, people expect to actively shape and create many aspects of their lives. Why would a teen constructing and sharing her life on YouTube shift from a new power model to an old power model upon entering the workforce? The answer is that teens entering the workforce as adults with a different preference for participation will change the power model in organizations, including community colleges.

New power favors informal, networked approaches to decision making. Organizational problems are solved without excessive oversight or bureaucracy. This ethos has at its core a belief in the power of innovation and networks to provide resources and services traditionally provided by big organizations. Old power notions of sequestered command and control are replaced by highly transparent interaction among large numbers of people who share more and more of their lives on social media. Affiliation is sought, but it is not enduring. New power advocates are quick to join and share with others, but they tend not to form long relationships with organizations. It is the ideas that serve as the force for banding together versus institutional loyalty or obligation.

What will this mean for community college leaders? There will be a compelling need to reframe and rethink relationships with faculty and staff. Power will need to be distributed throughout the organization, and employees will need to build and use capabilities they heretofore have not been called upon to use. Chief among them will be an understanding not only of internal operating dynamics but also external forces that shape institutional resources and direction. Perpetually sensing and responding to external demands and competition will no longer be the sole purview of a few at the top. Rather, there will be considerably greater complexity involved in identifying and tapping leadership capability both within and outside the institution as a means of advancing the vision and fulfilling the mission.

Redesigning Organizational Architecture

John Kotter[12] argues for an organizational architecture built on a dual system of operations. One part of the system is the traditional organizational hierarchy that keeps the organization running by maintaining basic operations and processes. The other focuses on innovation and is mobilized by individuals interested in ideation, problem solving, and testing solutions, yet knowing in advance that some will fail. This part of the organization creates new destinations and opportunities for growth. The system encourages crossover of employees between operations and innovation hubs through fluid projects that strategically draw personnel and expertise from different parts of the organization. Critical to its success are connections between innovators and operators to avoid duplication of effort and provide constant feedback to the system.[13]

For the dual system to work, employees must become comfortable with the fact that many, perhaps most, initiatives will fail. James Lorenson, president of Gogebic Community College, calls this "the fast fail."[14]

> Not everything will work. Learn from mistakes and move on. We need to develop different ways of looking at the issues and problems we try to solve. We can't take a year or two years to develop programs. We say we're responsive, but when you look at our actual timelines, we're not.

The key to the fast fail is learning from what did not work. Failure is a learning opportunity that can be remarkably beneficial if leaders and institutional teams embrace risk and become adept at perpetual ideation and testing of solutions that have the potential to bolster the institution's effectiveness.

Changing the architecture of community colleges also means jettisoning time-honored traditions. For example, the time frame of the academic semester, the fifteen-week course, the certification of learning through grades, and the definition of a credit are now challenged by sophisticated online education resources that deliver learning anytime, anyplace, anywhere. Colleges have become creative in offering courses online and in different formats to accommodate students (e.g., Bunker Hill Community College offered classes at midnight to accommodate student schedules).[15]

New processes are also evident in the Tennessee Technology Centers' use of competency-based curriculum. Rather than credit hours and seat time, programs follow a clock-hour format in which faculty instruct students over the course of the semester, allowing students to progress at a rate corresponding to the competencies they build.[16] Likewise, Western Governors University moves learners through courses and programs on the basis of demonstrated competency rather than accumulated seat time.[17] These innovations place the emphasis on students as the primary consumer of learning in contrast to the traditional emphasis on instructors and teaching. Students take center stage, and instructors assume the role of guides on the side.

Building Education Networks

If it is true, as many believe, that networked organizations are the wave of the future, the implication for leaders and college employees will be severe, and the disruption intense. Employee roles play out differently in a network than they do in a self-contained organization. No longer do academic departments and administrative units function as silos, nor can colleges silo themselves from organizations in the larger community. The integrating power of networks is illustrated by the Kresge Foundation in its Talent Dividend Prize competition.[18]

Colleges participating in the competition were able to enhance graduation rates through linkages forged with business and industry employers and K–12 schools. Employers working directly with college instructors in curriculum and program development mobilized students by connecting learning to the world of work. The cocreation of curricula is a sizeable step beyond current forms of academic "collaboration," such as program advisory board input and developing a curriculum (DACUM), because the focus is on creating programs and courses that simultaneously address current and anticipated employer needs and motivate students to learn. This type of collaborative programming moves key elements of learning from the classroom to the field to provide opportunities for authentic learning.[19]

Rethinking curricula and the process for curriculum development also means reexamining the meaning of applied degrees. The Lumina Foundation is currently working with colleges and universities to identify competencies for academic degrees through their Degree Qualifications Profile[20] project. Lumina's focus is on general education curricula, but a similar profile for applied degrees would be helpful to employers and career-bound students.

If the goal of an applied degree is employment, what do students need to learn, what skills do they need to develop to perform well in a specific job, and how can colleges optimally equip students with the competencies they need? The result may be a more malleable degree that provides for different skill sets customized to specific employer needs. Perhaps company sponsorship of degree completion would result in different tracks for completion. A new award designation may even be needed, such as a badge to demonstrate competency or some other type of "career credential."

As networks grow in importance, community colleges will likely need to change their internal organization architecture. Resource sharing will become increasingly important and positions may need to be restructured to facilitate knowledge transfer within and among organizations. In Central Queensland, Australia, the government improved response time to business and industry needs by merging all regional, publicly supported institutions of higher education. Beginning with curriculum mapping—with industry experts leading the way—curricula were revamped in career programs (refrigeration, engineering technologies, and licensed practical nurse [LPN] to registered nurse [RN]).[21]

Sharing expertise throughout a multiorganizational network helped to close gaps in the school-to-work pipeline. Undergirding the power of the network in this instance were shared data systems connecting multiple players—educational institutions, state agencies, and private industries—to the common goal of producing a competent workforce in support of shared individual, corporate, economic, and social goals.

RETHINKING MISSION AND CONTROL

Colleges rarely start with a blank slate when undertaking change. Existing structures and frameworks are remarkably resistant to modification—a reality that limits the extent and scope of change. Leaders and staff carry the baggage of past and present ways of doing things, and influencing new habits of thinking and acting within an organization is easier said than done. Leaders must find ways to free themselves from the chains of what they already know.[22] And there is no better place to start than understanding mission and control, which are deeply embedded in the culture of institutions.

Are radical shifts in the mission and control of community colleges likely to happen in the not-so-distant future? Think about the possibilities. Will community colleges remain stand-alone institutions offering a necessarily limited curriculum within a small geographical footprint? Probably not.

The University System of Georgia's State Board of Regents merged eight public colleges in 2013 to cut costs and simultaneously expand academic programs.[23] Will some colleges merge with K–12 school districts to create a seamless pathway to college? Jackson College in Michigan has embarked on this journey. When this happens, must organizational architecture and positions change to accommodate new players? You bet. Will it continue to be beneficial for community colleges to remain part of a state system of oversight when the majority of funding comes from other sources? Our colleges have become state-located in contrast to state-supported; why continue to operate on the state till? Some colleges may be able to bring in more dollars as autonomous free-standing institutions operating outside state control.

New thinking requires a fertile imagination, a capacity to see and pursue opportunity, and the wherewithal to embrace risk. To what extent do leaders—current and prospective—have the mettle to think differently and to guide institutions to a different future?

Reenvisioning Curricula

The shift to competency-based education is clearly a wave of the future for curricula. U.S. Secretary of Education Arne Duncan said

"Today's technology-enabled, information-rich, deeply interconnected world means learning not only can—but *should*—happen anywhere, anytime. We need to *recognize* [italics added for emphasis] these experiences, whether the environments are physical or online, and whether learning takes place in schools, colleges or adult education centers, or in afterschool, workplace, military or community settings."[24]

Still, colleges are constrained by federal financial aid regulations, and competency remains subject to variable definitions. Colleges and universities have a legally enforced near-monopoly over the production of credentials that are widely accepted for job entry or advanced education. Soft skills, which are developed largely outside formal classroom settings, are invaluable to employers and correlated with job success, but these skills rarely show up on a transcript. Résumés as a vehicle for presenting knowledge and skills are "flat" and difficult, if not impossible, to verify.[25] Additionally, knowledge is no longer confined to institutions of higher education given the availability and quality of online education resources.

New forms of credentialing are emerging. "We're already seeing the impact of alternative, industry-recognized credentials at sites such as www.topcoder.com, which has opened up a significant new path for computer programmers seeking to demonstrate skills that qualify them for good jobs with high-paying salaries at fast-growing companies like Google and Facebook."[26] Badges are being used to certify competence and to document learning. "One badge-based system, Smarterer (http://smarterer.com/about/how_it_works), tests users on a specific skill via multiple choice questions and awards a badge certifying how much they know."[27] The results of the test are measured against topic content (e.g., finance, software packages, etc.), and the Smarterer system then informs test-takers what they still need to learn to improve their mastery of the content. More than five hundred subjects are available on the system.

Although badge programs and other credentialing alternatives have not moved forward as expected, future-focused leaders need to determine what credentials—whether badges, certificates, degrees, or something to be developed—are relevant to the workforce and figure out how colleges can mesh newly identified credentials with traditional academic measures of learning.

Beyond formal education, how can colleges measure and reward lifelong learning that occurs on the job outside college walls? Some colleges have provided guarantees that graduates will have the skills employers need or the college will retrain them.[28] Leaders should be thinking beyond classroom programs, however, and focusing on what colleges can do to recognize what soldiers learn through training and experience, what caregivers learn through serving, and what employees learn on the job, then figuring out how this real learning can be applied to further education.

The future will require a collaborative approach to learning. Collaboration is necessary between colleges, employers, K–12 programs, and students. Leaders will need to get ahead of the change curve on curriculum design or face the prospect of being left behind.

As if this were not enough, what can colleges and leaders do to appropriately engage outside organizations in program and course creation? What is the optimal place for business and industry employers in curriculum mapping? Once seen as a local commodity, community colleges are now broadband systems connected to state and federal governments and sundry organizations around the world. They have an elastic nature that leaves them no option but to bend and stretch in tandem with the landscape around them.

Although the leadership literature purports that institutions are in constant pursuit of equilibrium and balance, Wheatley[29] indicates that, to the contrary, equilibrium is "the point in which a system has exhausted all of its capacity for change, done its work, and dissipated the productive capacity into useless entropy." This description does not paint a pretty picture of the ideal state for an organization holding to a constant state of equilibrium. To remain viable within a connected world, leaders and colleges must remain in a state of "continuous imbalance" so that the system has a chance to change and grow. Like walking down the aisle of a moving airplane, leaders must be able to perform well in a state of disequilibrium, or to mix the metaphor, be able to "play ball on running water."[30]

New Accountability Models

As though frame-breaking changes in organizational structure, curricula, and credentialing were not enough, new models of accountability and accreditation are evolving and will continue to do so. Educational attainment will be tracked and analyzed across the P–16 continuum and against standards created by public and private investors. West Virginia and Florida have invested in state-wide data systems that track students from the start of schooling in Pre-K through public schools and ultimately into college for those who pursue post-secondary education. Florida[31] links its P–20 data with workforce data to increase system-wide efficiencies. In this case, data informs policy for legislative funding and for continuing or changing programs, and community colleges play a linchpin role in the system. The linked data helps create efficiencies between agencies and highlights what is working in the various sectors. It is hard to argue with the numbers, and the transparency of the data provides motivation and increased urgency to change systems—a good example of distributed or networked power. Other burgeoning states in the data metrics arena, like West Virginia, are putting data systems in place to achieve their state master plan goals.[32]

Thirty-three states have implemented some form of performance-based funding.[33] These externally driven assessments of performance are challenging institutional conceptions of success and changing the turf on which resource decisions are made. The national college rating systems currently under development at the federal level decidedly elevates the role of external stakeholders, and ultimately, as with other ranking systems (e.g., *U.S. News & World Report*), competition will drive attention to pricing and student success.

The overarching goal of these systems is to ensure that college performance meets real-world expectations. The implications for institutions and leaders are clear: it will be necessary to relentlessly communicate the community college mission to policy makers in their language, to involve policy makers in the development of performance criteria, and to consistently measure and report on consensual performance indicators. The battle will be uphill and on an uneven playing field. Most policy makers were educated in four-year colleges and universities and, therefore, have a limited understanding of what it means to be an academically challenged student in need of different support structures.

Changing accountability mandates are not limited to policy makers and government agencies. In the private sector, granting agencies, foundations, and individual donors are supplanting state support as a primary source of revenue for community colleges. Resources from these providers, not unlike governmental support, come with strings attached; these outside stakeholders expect a voice in resource decisions and operations in return for support.

Private support is essential if community colleges are to maintain open access and robust portfolios of academic programs. The give-and-take nature of such support, however, poses a question for leaders: Is private support central or peripheral to mission and core values? If the answer is "yes," all parties benefit. If the answer is "no," a determination must be made as to the value of support if it does not align with mission and values.

New Approaches to Communication

The importance of how information is framed and presented to internal and external audiences has long been recognized, yet leaders still make missteps and gaffes, particularly when describing institutional strategic decisions, resource needs, and outcomes. In a fast-changing landscape it will be increasingly important for leaders to frame change in ways that internal and external constituencies can understand.

The way in which change is framed will set the stage for expectations and action. Black and Gregerson[34] describe the power of one—underscoring how critical it is to reach people on a personal level to obtain buy-in for change. A key step along the way is to establish an urgency for change that is undeniable, clearly understood, and acted upon by employees. Communication that can effectively be used to instill a sense of urgency is one of the great management challenges in community colleges today.

It is clear that developing leaders with solid communication skills throughout the organization will take on increasing importance in networked organizations because this shift effectively moves the locus for communication from senior administrators to employees distributed across all parts of the organization. As an example, a different pattern of communication opens up when employees are intentionally prepped to understand common issues and to ably communicate those issues to an intended audience. James Lorenson reflected on the importance of open communication with the following reflection:

> The people we often spend the least time with are classified employees. So now we spend lots of time with our custodians and our support staff, so that they know as much as anyone else on campus about whose office is where, where Student Services are, where Financial Aid is, and the sort of people working in each area. When someone comes and asks for help or directions, it's part of their job to set the broom aside or move from their desk and take the individual to the office. Custodians aren't just being trained on how to be good custodians. They're being trained to be good ambassadors for the college.
>
> Likewise our staff are privy to and are primed on strategic information that is vital to college operations—information on appropriations, legislative issues, policy issues in Lansing and Washington and so forth. If a staff member should see one of our legislators at a county fair or at a meeting, he or she can speak intelligently about issues affecting Gogebic Community College. Why should I or the deans be the only ones who can speak to people about the issues confronting the college?[35]

This approach to networking underscores the need to have a viable system for framing and communicating information throughout the college. It also illustrates that *everyone* can and should be involved in telling the college story.

Just like Oz playing the man behind the curtain focusing people's attention in specific ways, so too must leaders help focus employees to pay attention to what is most important for the institution. Traditional leaders spend a significant amount of time crafting strategic initiatives and plans for the college, yet they typically spend a relatively small portion of time managing the message of change. Here, the process takes on more importance than change itself. Think of what would be possible if leaders focused on restructuring organizational reporting by creating internal networks in which staff learned together and interacted to facilitate the process of change. A structure of this type would provide key information to staff to see and do what needs to be done. This type of framing would occur in multiple parts of the institution simultaneously and create a ripple effect for change.

IMPLICATIONS FOR LEADERS

What are the implications of these practices for leaders? For starters, the next generation of leaders will need to embrace Janusian thinking and vision. They will need to see how conflicting truths coexist and how simultaneously contradictory needs can be met. The ability to bring seemingly disparate groups together from within and outside the organization is critical to success in networked organizations. Leaders need to be able to work in dual, or even treble, systems with ease. Multisystem agility makes it possible to effectively communicate consistent messages to different stakeholders. The communication medium required for different audiences may vary, but the underlying message must be the same.

As we have argued throughout the book, it is important to borrow tactics from other sectors as a means for mobilizing change. It is also important to recognize that tools and tactics from other organizations cannot be brought to community colleges without customization to mission, culture, and organizational goals. Leaders need to be skillful in transporting and translating external practices to staff. Resistance builds when staff cannot see the relevance of change or fear how it will impact their work.

Here is where leaders can use data and analytics to make the case for change. Facing the challenge of a gap in educational delivery to urban and rural regions of the state, Glenn DuBois, Chancellor of the Virginia Community College System (VCCS), used information from the state data bank to build a case for alternative delivery systems in sparsely and heavily populated regions of the state. Demographic data revealed stark differences in educational need and aspirations for rural and urban populations. Only 19 percent of the population in the rural horseshoe had a bachelor's degree or higher, putting the region at the bottom of the nation in postsecondary education attainment.

The urban crescent was exactly the opposite—if the crescent were its own state, it would rank second nationally in college attainment with 38 percent of the population having a bachelor's degree or higher.[36] Using this information, a Rural Virginia Horseshoe Initiative was launched in 2013.[37] Framing the community college story differed by region because college-aged youth in rural Virginia did not have sufficient information or background experience to access postsecondary education, let alone complete a degree. The community college story had to be presented to them in an entirely different manner than their urban counterparts. The message for leaders: frame the community college story in ways that match message with context, constituency needs, and expectations and preferences for communication.

Widely sharing information breaks down silos. Institutions and leaders are operating in a complex, fast-change landscape. It is difficult, if not impossible, for decision makers—individual or group—to get their arms around simultaneously occurring events and understand their long-range consequences. The more widely information is shared and the more heads at work on a problem or issue, the better the result. Simply stated, leaders will have the greatest odds of success by using the full array of talent available both inside and outside the institution to fulfill the mission and to remain competitive in the transformed industry of higher education. The question is how to develop leaders with this type of understanding and skill?

A logical first step would be to assess our current model for developing leaders and to honestly identify what is and is not working. Next, we need to think about alternative means for developing leaders who can navigate, with eyes wide open, the challenge of leading complex institutions in a turbulent landscape.

DEVELOPING LEADERS: TODAY'S MODEL

Most of the responsibility for developing community college leaders is left to doctoral programs in higher education or community college leadership and national organizations like the League for Innovation, the Association of Community College Trustees, and the American Association for Community Colleges. Several states have established community college leadership academies (e.g., Alabama, Iowa, Massachusetts, and Virginia), and research universities offer specialized training programs (such as Harvard's Institute for New Presidents and Executive Leadership programs and Bryn Mawr's HERS) for community college leaders and aspiring leaders. Typically these programs are centered on the illustration of current best practices (cynically referred to as "the old guys telling war stories") in contrast to knowledge development and skill training for innovation. All things considered, the Achilles' heel of these programs is their emphasis on staid leadership practices that worked in the past but provide virtually no assurance of working in the future.

On-the-job training augmented by "seat learning" in doctoral programs continues to be the primary vehicle for professional development for the vast majority of community college leaders. The doctorate has become the de facto credential for community college leadership, with 80 percent of sitting presidents holding a doctorate.[38] Doctoral programs do not necessarily convey great secrets about leadership, but they are often viewed as a test of endurance—proof that an individual can follow through with a long-term commitment.

The efficacy of graduate programs in education was called into question by Arthur Levine[39] in a treatise calling out programs for ill-defined curricula, reliance on rote learning versus authentic learning, and formats that did not accommodate adult learners. In response to this report, a research project on graduate education was developed at the Carnegie Foundation for Teaching and Learning that led to the creation of the Carnegie Project on the Education Doctorate (CPED)[40] involving a consortium of eighty colleges and schools of education.

Phase I of the project (2007–2010) involved twenty-five institutions that worked on definitions of the professional EdD and design concepts. Phase II (2011–2013) created a CPED framework and admitted twenty-five additional member institutions. Phase III (2014–present) has admitted thirty-seven new members to the consortium and continues to refine research communities to disseminate best practices. Nonetheless, member colleges persist in tweaking a professional doctorate that may meet the needs of some of today's colleges or those individuals just beginning the degree process. What about preparing the leaders needed to upend the status quo in community college education? Will these programs be of any value or service to those who already have a doctorate and a leadership role but are altogether ill-equipped for the transformation journey?

Although earning a doctorate can provide a meaningful learning experience for aspiring leaders, the shortcomings of academic credentials as preparation for leadership was acknowledged by American Association of Community Colleges (AACC) in 2005 when it created Competencies for Community College Leaders. AACC's *Leading Forward* initiative used focus groups with current leaders to devise a six-point list of competencies.

In 2013, these competencies were updated to recognize leadership needs throughout the college and now distinguish developmental needs for emerging leaders, new presidents, and presidents in the field longer than three years.[41] The caution with any type of a list created by consensus is that groupthink may constrain innovative ideas about new ways to develop leaders. At their core, the AACC competencies remain a listing of generic skills for leaders and suggestions for how to build these skills.

Reviewing the skills identified for each of the competencies developed by AACC, let us consider how they might be enhanced to focus on the future:

- "Organizational Strategy: *An effective community college leader promotes the success of all students, strategically improves the quality of the institution, and sustains the community college mission based on knowledge of the organization, its environment, and future trends.*"[42]

  What mirrors our argument about building a capacity for leading in turbulence in this competency is the need to be forward-thinking and to embrace a culture of change and risk. However, the language in this competency assumes continuation of the current architecture for operation—an architecture that is modeled on best practices. Merely improving leadership practice using incremental change will not be enough in our current change environment. There is no mention in this competency of how to change organizational culture in a way that unleashes the creative potential of leaders.

- "Institutional Finance, Research, Fundraising, and Resource Management: *An effective community college leader equitably and ethically sustains people, processes, and information as well as physical and financial assets to fulfill the mission, vision, and goals of the community college.*"[43]

  Clear in this competency is the need to understand and use institutional performance data. Leaders must also effectively fund-raise to augment the bottom line, but this assumes that colleges merely need more money to improve performance. The definition provided overlooks the pressing need for colleges to more efficiently and strategically use the funds they currently have. This competency acknowledges the importance of teams being created to do the work, but the level and location of these teams is not clear. Given the excessive reliance on the hierarchy in our colleges, it is not unreasonable to assume that "teams" may refer to those at the top of the organization. This would leave instructors and support staff out of the loop on resource management and performance assessment. Allocating scarce resources creates winners and losers, and hence, conflict. Reliance on the hierarchy may increase administrative efficiency, but it comes with a cost. Large numbers of employees with a stake in the institution are left out of the decision process and resist rather than move with change.

- "Communication: *An effective community college leader uses clear listening, speaking, and writing skills to engage in honest, open dialogue at all levels of the college and its surrounding community; promotes the success of all students; ensures the safety and security of students and the surrounding college community; and sustains the community college mission.*"[44]

The manner in which leaders communicate with key stakeholders, how they tell the story of new initiatives, how they convey a commitment to student success, and how they communicate with network partners makes the difference between success and failure. The skills in this competency identify discrete components of communication, but the importance of framing the message is lost. Also, not evident is the role of social capital in communication. Social capital is built via IOUs between people who rely on trust and a belief in common goals. Not only does this mean listening to others, but it also means understanding what the real issues are and not merely what is stated. Levels of social capital influence the type and range of communication that occurs.

- "Collaboration: *An effective community college leader develops and maintains responsive, cooperative, mutually beneficial, and ethical internal and external relationships that nurture diversity, promote the success of all students, and sustain the community college mission.*"[45]

Collaboration is built on trust and mutual need. Creating a climate in which people want to work together requires recognition of the value of individual contributions. Historic conceptions and misconceptions of shared governance, coupled with imperfect implementation, have, in effect, created a vast chasm between faculty and administration. If not through shared governance as it has been traditionally conceived and executed, then how can well-executed networked systems of leadership function to accomplish the mission and achieve the goals of student success?

- "Community College Advocacy: *An effective community college leader understands, commits to, and advocates for the mission, vision, and goals of the community college on the local, state, and national level.*"[46]

A key role of community college leaders is to represent the college to external audiences, yet what is inferred in this competency is engagement in the policy process at different levels of government. How policy issues are defined and how legislative agendas are set depend on how effectively community college leaders depict their needs. What is missing in this competency, however, is a need to advocate with entities that may not be central to resource procurement. Many states have P–16 or P–20 councils and espouse a need for alignment of educational outcomes, but few are successful. Advocacy should involve collaborating across the aisle with P–12 colleagues working with the Common Core Standards to ensure smooth school-to-college-to-work transitions. Community college leaders need to think about what they are advocating for—market share or something larger and more closely aligned with the core mission of student success?

Even more important is the matter of mission. Mission creep and perpetual accretion are no longer sustainable. More is not necessarily better. Figuring out what is mission-critical and what is not, then determining what can be abandoned, what can be developed or enhanced through resource reallocation, and what can be outsourced to other providers will be an increasingly critical undertaking for community college leaders. We cannot emphasize this point strongly enough because elimination has proven to be a much more difficult undertaking for community college leaders than addition or substitution.

New leaders are faced with drinking from a fire hydrant of issues, and how they deal with this is influenced by the skills they have—or have not—acquired along the way. For example, the American Council on Education's periodic survey of presidents asks what they felt unprepared for in their role. In 2012, the top five responses were:

1. Fund Raising (49.3%)
2. Capital Improvement Projects (31.2%)
3. Risk Management/Legal Issues (25.6%)
4. Budget/Financial Management (23.5%)
5. Government Relationships (23.3%)[47]

Note how many of these issues focused on finance and politics. Budget issues on campus stem, for the most part, from changes in government funding—both for colleges and for students. Given the precipitous drop in government funding that community colleges have experienced in recent years, it is easy to see how AACC came up with its list of competencies focused on advocacy and collaboration. Consider, as well, that AACC constructed its competencies on the basis of dialogue with currently serving presidents in institutions with traditional structures and processes—an approach to research that would not be likely to encourage out-of-the-box thinking.

Further, the AACC competencies were designed to fit the boundaried structure of community colleges as self-contained organizations. It is no surprise then that absent from the AACC competencies would be an understanding of the interdependencies that exist among networked organizations and how those interdependencies will shape the future.[48]

The rapid development of community colleges was the catalyst needed to open access to higher education. These early colleges were agile, but they took on many of the problems of complex organizations as they grew and matured. Bureaucracy and hierarchy became entrenched, eliminating the ability to react quickly. Today's leaders know how to resolve problems of the past. As Kotter argues, "We've learned how to execute change by adding task forces, tiger teams, project management departments, and executive sponsors for new initiatives."[49] But silos and hierarchies constrain the ability of leaders to deal with fast-paced change. The time has arrived to rethink leaders and leadership— who the leaders should be, where to find them, and how to develop them. No longer can the Lone Ranger come in to save the day. We need to think differently about leaders and leadership.

THINKING DIFFERENTLY ABOUT
LEADER DEVELOPMENT

Let us step back for a minute and envision a new horizon for community college leadership development. Throughout this book we have argued that old ways of doing business will not work any longer, which implies that traditional approaches to leadership development are not going to cut it either. Here we propose alternative ways of thinking about how to develop tomorrow's leaders—leaders we refer to as *networked leaders*.

Some caveats: *First*, it is important to recognize that strategies for leader development will vary in effectiveness for individuals and institutions. Context matters and so, too, do personality traits and individual capabilities. Just as learning needs to be individualized for students, so too do development strategies for leaders.

Second, any discussion about strategies for developing leaders needs to begin with a general statement on leadership which, for our purposes, is something that occurs at all levels in an institution regardless of position or title. Leadership is collaborative, contextual, fluid, and multidimensional.[50] Leadership must be looked at as a responsibility borne not solely by one person or a group, but by many within the institution.

Third, when we talk about leadership development, we are referring to strategies to help individuals develop capabilities that we believe are necessary to transform community colleges and lead them into the future.

Developing leaders must become an integral part of the dynamic enterprise that is the community college. Deep change is underway and the training needed to get leaders ready for a different future needs to be carefully considered. The health-care industry faced similar challenges a generation ago. Rising costs, new systems and regulations, and stringent assessment procedures added complexity to health-care management and brought the industry to a threshold of change never before experienced. The industry used the crisis as an opportunity to change traditional practices.[51]

Now decision making in health-care organizations is made closer to the ground level with nurses taking on increased responsibility and receiving recognition for leadership on the floor. Data management systems are streamlined to provide common source information for multiple professionals working with a patient. Cost-saving methods are embedded into everyday practices, and processes are constantly evaluated for ways to improve efficiency. The upshot is new programs to develop skills in aspiring leaders and a deep commitment to succession planning in the health-care industry. We must make similar changes in the community college sector.

Rather than grooming a successor within each college, top leaders and boards should consider grooming a stable of leaders primed to take over leadership positions at all levels in a college. Not all trained within a college will advance in-house, but another institution, most likely in the community college sector, will benefit from the investment in leadership training. Leaders may argue against widespread employee grooming for fear of losing their investment, but placement of former employees in new institutions builds the corps of leaders and strengthens the industry as a whole—not to mention adding strong links within the community college network.

What might training for the next generation of community college leaders look like? An array of modalities are possible ranging from preparing current students for next-generation leadership roles to accessing talent and ideas from industries outside education to shaking up graduate education programs.

Preparing Current Students for Leadership Roles

Community colleges enroll the most diverse student body in all of higher education, yet this diversity is not evident in leadership ranks. The percentage of leaders of color in community colleges has flatlined for the past twenty years.[52] The numbers are telling: 45 percent of community college students are students of color[53]; 19 percent are faculty of color[54]; and 15 percent of chief academic officers are people of color.[55] Almost nine out of ten community college presidents (87 percent) are white.

As institutions of opportunity, community colleges have fostered a reputation for being welcoming institutions to students of color, particularly those students entering college underprepared for college-level work. But the loss of minority representation in leadership positions begins early in the pipeline with administrators and faculty of color not at equity levels relative to students of color. Picture this in Figure 4.1.

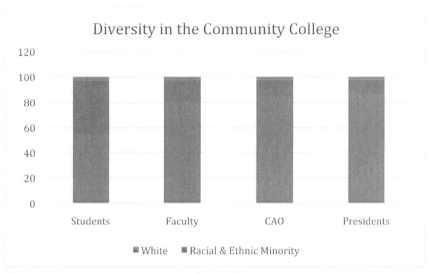

Figure 4.1. Diversity Representation in Community Colleges

What is missing in this portrait? Who is not present the further one moves up the organizational chart? Whose voices are not heard?

We rarely target community college students when cultivating leaders, but many sitting leaders have community college student roots. Selectively opening leadership opportunities to current students—especially students of color—would be a way to diversify leadership ranks in community colleges. Granted, this approach to leader development is long term, but without it nothing will change. Providing opportunities for students to experience what it means to be a leader can instill in them a goal of returning to the community college to pursue a career at the conclusion of their academic career. Student leadership programs are on the increase nationwide,[56] and we can use this to our advantage in developing future leaders.

The location of 60 percent of community colleges in rural areas creates an added incentive to selectively groom currently enrolled students for leadership. Rural community colleges tend to promote more from within the college given the difficulty of recruiting leaders to more remote locations.[57] Additionally, students attending rural colleges often do so because of an affinity for their communities and convenient access to higher education.

Rural communities with high poverty, low educational attainment, and scant business enterprises require leaders with special skills—skills that may be most fully developed in youth growing up in these rural communities, their home communities. Targeting currently enrolled students for future leaders is a win–win.

Identifying Hidden Talent

Leader development programs typically operate on the basis of supervisors selecting employees for participation, yet selection becomes a self-fulfilling prophecy when supervisors pick the same kinds of individuals over and over for leadership training. This process prompts several questions: Who are we missing when we rely solely on this form of selection? What potential is lost when we focus solely on people more highly placed in the institution in contrast to focusing on people in positions (i.e., classified staff) not commonly associated with leadership? What potential is lost when we open leadership opportunity to those who "look and act like leaders" in contrast to those who may not look like leaders but bring diverse skill sets to the table?

Consider the extent to which classified staff are overlooked when selecting personnel for leadership development.[58] We can no longer continue to rely on a select pool of employee types to draft into leadership. The time has come to broaden and diversify the pool to include the full spectrum of staff working toward achieving the community college mission.

A good way to find hidden talent is through cross-positional and cross-unit project teams or committees. Leaders should periodically check into the work of these teams to learn who has contributed to outcomes and shown potential for leadership. Observing project teams at work provides a good litmus test for identifying informal leaders currently in place at our colleges. Another source of hidden talent is staff involved with professional and community groups outside work. Many hold leadership positions in these organizations and have leadership skills that have gone untapped in the workplace.

Think about how the leadership skills involved in leading a community fund drive for United Way build expertise in organizational strategy, how service as treasurer for a church group creates fiscal skills, how being the social media organizer for Big Brothers/Big Sisters provides expertise on communication skills, and how working on a community effort to combat hunger hones interpersonal and intergroup negotiation skills. Unfortunately all too many sitting college presidents know little to nothing about what college employees do beyond the 9-to-5 workday. We need to capitalize on the skills employees are developing outside the college environment.

We know that sitting leaders will readily talk about how they arrived at their positions, many quite by "accident."[59] These individuals were not necessarily thinking of top-level positions along the way. Often they were the good soldiers who conscientiously performed their jobs as faculty or staff members, and they faithfully carried out other tasks or responsibilities when called upon to do so. We know who these people are on campus. They are the ones people look to when something needs to get done.

What happens, however, when instead of thinking of these people as merely worker bees, we find ways to involve them in organized training to become future leaders? With intentional effort, faculty and staff on the ground floor and in middle ranks can morph into leaders, but we need to get to them early to stave off complacency and the development of bad habits. Further, we need to enculturate a passion for innovation and methods that can improve the organization in creative ways. Community colleges can no longer afford to overlook "doers" and "thought leaders." Indeed, we must provide them with real opportunities for leadership.

Leadership Academies

A number of community college leadership academies have sprung up over the years.[60] Typically, these academies have relied on university faculty with connections to community colleges or a cadre of experienced community college presidents. Some community college organizations also provided short-term leadership training. Although academies and training programs have provided baseline training for aspiring leaders, what is missing is a focus on innovation and creative practices.

Infusing existing academies with a learning experience focused on transformation and alternative ways of thinking about the future for community colleges is an approach with considerable promise, yet it is hard to conceive of such an approach when relying predominately on current practice as the development agenda for prospective leaders. Although some skills are certainly transferable from current practice, new skills are required to lead in today's and tomorrow's environment. How then can leadership academies be enhanced to address these needs?

One option is to deliver leadership training preparation through private companies offering a unique learning experience. Decoupling training from current practice and privatizing it can perhaps provide the fresh space and tools needed. As Kotter[61] argues, "Innovation requires risk, people who are willing to think outside the box, perspectives from multiple silos, and more."

Private academies can create a new forum for development and along with it, access to different types of networks. Not being linked to a college does not mean that the context of the community college will be ignored when academies are privatized. The skill sets delivered by these companies could be certified by college governing boards and recognized as providing training of the order required to prepare the next generation of leaders.

Training provided by private companies might concentrate on skills for creating and leading transformation, such as disruptive innovation, data analytics and business intelligence, culture change, creating and operating in networks, and generating new revenue streams. Tomorrow's leaders will need to learn how to communicate with different generations of workers and across different constituency arenas.

At least five generations of workers will be present in the workplace of the future, each with different preferences and expectations for communication. How do leaders effectively communicate with multiple generations? As to communication with external constituencies, long-standing interactions with business and industry will need to move past partnerships based solely on workforce development. Leaders will need to learn how to leverage relationships to change funding streams, policy, and the manner in which students are educated. New leaders will need to learn how to build coalitions and shape the policy dialogue to achieve desired results.

Shaking up Doctoral Programs

Historically, the doctoral degree has been viewed as an entry ticket into top-level leadership positions. We know, however, that the PhD is considered too theoretical, and the EdD has issues of respectability in some circles. Moreover, some educational doctorate programs have chosen to depart from a practice-based emphasis and instead mimic the PhD, often with questionable results. Most doctoral programs rely on a set curriculum and dated views of leadership that retard college progress toward the future.[62] Yes, there is value in these programs. They help prospective leaders learn how organizations work if, and this is a big if, they stretch beyond current boundaries.

So, what is missing in the current curriculum? We have to adjust the manner in which graduate programs allow for authentic, outcomes-based leadership development. The increase in online options for graduate work, a focus on customized programs for community college leadership, and the creation of executive-oriented offerings present a glimmer of what is possible. What if we started to offer credit for experience? How about changing to modules for course work in contrast to fifteen weeks of seat time in a graduate course? How can we provide the worldview necessary to become conversant with best practices beyond institutional borders?

In *Re-Visioning Community Colleges*, Sydow and Alfred[63] analyzed a bold experiment in Australia to merge various sectors of higher education from the two-year technical and further education (TAFE) colleges up to the "sandstones" or most elite of their universities. The objective was not only to reduce costs but, more important, to rework higher education deliverables with a focus on credentials relevant to students and employers.

One way that our graduate programs can meaningfully change is through the use of stackable certificates. For example, offering a graduate-level College Teaching Certificate can deliver two important outcomes. First, it can engage faculty in leadership. Second, it can help leaders understand the academic context for student success and how students best learn. Training of this type can also provide aspiring leaders with a head start on the doctorate.

Leadership academies can play a role by offering transferable graduate credit for work on a College Leadership Certificate. Another type of certificate could be a Research and Data Analytics Certificate to develop skills for transforming big data into business intelligence. Add to this a Policy certificate that incorporates strategic planning, policy development, and fund development, and one can see how modules stack up to produce a graduate degree.

A final capstone project could yield a result that is actually useful instead of a solely research-driven dissertation that has no utility beyond its status as the primary criterion for degree completion. Instead of a test of endurance, doctoral programs need to focus on student learning and provide a level of customization necessary to prepare learners for a variety of leadership roles.

To meaningfully engage learners in the craft of leadership, it is important to employ graduate instructors who are innovative thinkers and to bring in leaders with substantial experience in community colleges and a track record of innovation to serve as affiliated faculty or coteachers. Teaching future leaders about the unique organizational context that is the community college, and its enormous potential for advancing public good, is one of the most important outcomes to be accomplished through graduate programs.

Existing programs clearly have strengths, but how can we leverage these programs to foster change in how we think about community colleges? How might governing boards adjust requirements for what new leaders must know and be able to do? We know that degrees have been the collateral needed to make the cut for top-level positions,[64] and increasingly for mid-level positions.[65] How might we change the focus from merely obtaining a graduate degree to developing the competencies and demonstrating the learning outcomes that are achieved through the degree? Competency is fast becoming the new standard of learning at the undergraduate level, so why not apply the concept of competency to the training of leaders at the graduate level?

Leadership Fellows

Job shadowing is a typical component of existing leadership programs, such as the American Council on Education Fellows program. However, the fellows program focuses specifically on leadership at the executive level. This type of preparation could extend to other leadership levels, including the department chair. The basis of most fellows programs is pairing aspiring leaders with senior leaders at other institutions to provide mentoring and a glimpse into what the role looks and feels like on a day-to-day basis. Fellows see firsthand the responsibilities of the position in a different institutional context, and they begin to identify the skill sets that they will need to develop in preparation for a career in executive leadership. But how do we move this concept forward given the specific leadership needs of our colleges?

One way would be to provide shadowing opportunities with business, industry, health, and not-for-profit organizations. Having an aspiring leader shadow a leader in a different type of organization would provide a number of benefits. First, fellows would gain a perspective on the knowledge and skills that future employers of community college students will require; this awareness can be used to reshape the community college curriculum. Second, fellows would obtain different perspectives on management and leadership in different industries and cultures. Finally, fellows would take an important first step toward building relationships across sectors that could prove useful for establishing short- and long-term strategic partnerships, for example, student internships.

Opportunities for cross-sector fellows are virtually limitless. Fellows might be placed in governmental offices, nongovernmental agencies, and policy associations. Think of the advantages for community college fellows in learning from the inside about the policies guiding student financial aid and accountability metrics. And the benefit is reciprocal; in true give-and-take fashion, the fellow would provide the host organization with an on-the-ground perspective of implications for the implementation of policies and programs.

Community colleges would benefit by developing programs that allow current employees to shadow high-performance employees at different levels, both in-house and in different institutions and organizations. This type of job shadowing can provide valuable cross-functional knowledge to help inform leadership practice. Programs can be structured to act like finishing schools for mid-level leaders. The military[66] and FBI[67] serve as useful models because these organizations have long taken the role of leader development quite seriously. All individuals serving in the military and FBI are exposed to core values and leadership principles from their first day of hire. Continuous evaluation provides an early indication of those with aspirations and the talent to advance.

Industry Professionals Outside Education

More common in recent years has been the arrival of leaders in community colleges from business, military, health organizations, and elected office. Community colleges leaders of the future will need to log similar experiences and possess some of the same background characteristics of leaders outside education. Currently about 42 percent of community college leaders have spent part of their career outside higher education.[68] These nonacademic experiences provide critical background and insights into best practices for innovation, yet a tripping point for some leaders coming from outside the sector has been the difficulty they experience as newcomers to the academic culture.[69]

Nonacademic leaders are used to quick actions in response to needs, and they do not always understand the slower pace of academic governance. Key, then, is how to use to full advantage the strengths of nonacademic leaders in a culture of shared governance. Ultimately, the academic culture will change over time given the influence of nontraditional leaders, and how we think of shared governance will likewise change. The counterproductive us-versus-them mind-set that is too often a by-product of shared governance will ultimately be remedied by progressive leaders who will rely more on relationships and networks than checks and balances to advance institutional goals.

The transition of leaders coming to our colleges from outside education can be made easier if they have a grounding in the mission and philosophy of community colleges. Pulling these potential leaders into the community college sphere in advance through work on advisory boards or governing boards is one way to provide exposure to values and culture. Contextual experience of this type exposes aspiring leaders to the academic culture and helps them to learn ways of working within the culture while changing it. Hard-charging change agents are short-lived if they do not figure out effective ways to deal with academe's entrenched resistance to change.

Creating a boot camp for introducing the historic legacy of the community college could also help to bridge the gap. This early and intense immersion would be akin to teaching aspiring, nontraditional leaders the secret handshake and rituals of the campus, but, more important, it would expose these new leaders to key values and the language used in-house. Outside leaders and, indeed, all leaders, need to figure out how to honor the past while advancing on the future. As in any change environment, relationship building is essential.

Leadership Development for Boards

The leadership of governing boards is valuable in ways that extend well beyond presidential selection and termination. Beyond hiring and firing the president, they act on resource allocation, strategic direction, and policy. Although board members may bring with them leadership experience from other sectors, most do not have formal training or experience in leading community colleges. And although boards are usually provided training to ensure that they are able to perform their primary (e.g., fiduciary) responsibilities, and some members may pursue training through an association such as the Association of Governing Boards (AGB) or the Association of Community College Trustees (ACCT), critical gaps remain that could help board members to better understand their role as leaders and the role of the leaders they hire.

Board members are selected or elected on the basis of their experience in business or politics, but they need to understand academic cultures, in general, and the specific contextual environment of community colleges. The decisions made by boards have far-reaching consequences, particularly in the fast-changing landscape that community colleges currently occupy. Beyond understanding the basics of community college mission and structure, boards must possess the knowledge and foresight to lead institutions in achieving their mission in a different future. This task cannot be accomplished solely inside institutional walls. In many instances, external expertise is required and at question is where to acquire it beyond traditional sources such as AGB and ACCT.

SUMMING UP

Current leaders are well aware that issues of mission, resource procurement, and accountability for student success are not going away. In considering how to prepare leaders for the future, several crucial points emerge. Tomorrow's leaders must know how to work with data, but to do so, they need to make the invisible visible. Interpreting statistics on how students move through programs and classes, the barriers students face financially and academically, and key pressure points for failure or success require leaders to give life to numbers. Moreover, there is a palpable vision that must be created of what a college would look like when operating at optimum.

This vision, which reposes in the future, must be brought to the present and conveyed in ways that parties internal and external to the institution can understand. Campus communities are hungry for a vision that they can embrace and follow, but if leaders can not convey a vision of the future that others can buy into, no one will follow. Worse yet, if leaders cannot tell the community college story, someone else will, and community colleges may not like the ending.

The practice of promoting from within the community college—one out of three sitting presidents was promoted from within[70]—has perpetuated the culture and the players. This pattern of hiring can be akin to striking a Faustian bargain because those promoted from within may not bring with them fresh ideas or new ways of seeing problems.

The tendency of governing boards to look for experienced candidates may also be a limiting factor for bringing new blood into leadership. All too often, recycled presidents bring the same practices used at their last institution to their new gig. The background experience of college presidents dictates what they see as important and how they make decisions.[71]

More entrepreneurs, venture capitalists, systems engineers, and others with divergent skill sets in the ranks of leadership would add considerable value to the enterprise as a whole. The clear message and challenge for governing boards is to reconceptualize the definition of an effective leader and the attributes of leadership in a way that would be most beneficial to the college and its capacity for mission fulfillment. The strategies outlined previously can help colleges begin the important journey of finding and developing leaders for tomorrow.

NOTES

1. Arne Duncan, "Digital Badges for Learning," Remarks at the 4th Annual Launch of the MacArthur Foundation Digital Media and Lifelong Learning Competition, September 5, 2011, http://www.ed.gov/news/speeches/digital-badges-learning.

2. Adrianna Kezar, *How Colleges Change: Understanding, Leading, and Enacting Change* (New York: Routledge, 2013).

3. Pamela L. Eddy, "Changing of the Guard in Community Colleges: The Role of Leadership Development," in *Rethinking Leadership in a Complex, Multicultural, and Global Environment: New Concepts and Models for Higher Education.* ed. Adrianna Kezar (Sterling, VA: Stylus Press, 2009), 185–211.

4. Alfred, "Leaders, Leveraging, and Abundance," 118.

5. Adam Bryant, "Google's Quest to Build a Better Boss," *New York Times,* March 12, 2011, http://www.nytimes.com/2011/03/13/business/13hire .html?pagewanted=1&_r=2&.

6. "Leading the Four Generations at Work," *American Management Association*, November 6, 2014, http://www.amanet.org/training/articles/Leading-the-Four-Generations-at-Work.aspx.

7. Jeremy Heimans and Henry Timms, "Understanding 'New Power,'" *Harvard Business Review* 92, no. 12 (2014): 48–56.

8. Heimans and Timms, "Understanding 'New Power.'"

9. Heimans and Timms, "Understanding 'New Power,'" 48.

10. Heimans and Timms, "Understanding 'New Power,'" 48.

11. Bertrand Russell, *Power: A New Social Analysis* (London: Allen and Unwin, 1938), 23.

12. Kotter, *Accelerate.*

13. Karl E. Weick, "Educational Organizations as Loosely Coupled Systems," *Administrative Science Quarterly* (1976): 1–19.

14. Interview with James Lorenson, Gogebic Community College, Ironwood, MI, August 26, 2013.

15. "At Bunker Hill Community College, Some Classes Will Start at 11:45 P.M." *Chronicle of Higher Education,* July 16, 2009, http://chronicle.com/article/At-Bunker-Hill-Community/47896.

16. *A Working Model for Student Success: The Tennessee Technology Centers* (Washington, DC: Complete College America, n.d.), http://www .completecollege.org/docs/Tennessee%20Technology%20Centers-%20A%20 Preliminary%20Case%20Study(1).pdf.

17. Western Governors University, "The WGU Experience," http://www .wgu.edu/are_you_wgu/index.

18. CEOs for Cities, "The Talent Dividend™," http://www.ceosforcities.org/ city-dividends/talent.

19. Marilyn M. Lombardi, "Authentic Learning for the 21st Century: An Overview," (Educause Learning Initiatives Paper 1, May 2007), http://net.edu cause.edu/ir/library/pdf/ELI3009.pdf.

20. Cliff Adelman, Peter Ewell, Paul Gaston, and Carol Geary Schneider, "Degree Qualifications Profile" (Lumina Foundation, 2014), http://www.lumina foundation.org/resources/dqp.

21. Debbie Sydow and Richard Alfred, *Re-visioning Community Colleges: Positioning for Innovation* (Lanham, MD: Rowman & Littlefield Publishers, Inc., 2013).

22. J. Stewart Black and Hal B. Gregerson, *It Starts with One: Changing Individuals Changes Organizations*, 2nd ed. (Upper Saddle River, NJ: Pearson Education, Inc., 2008).

23. Laura Diamond, "Historic Vote Merges Eight Georgia Colleges into Four," *The Atlanta Journal-Constitution*, January 13, 2013, http://www.ajc.com/news/news/local/regents-give-final-ok-to-merge-georgia-colleges/nTqH4/.

24. Duncan, "Digital Badges for Learning."

25. Saga Briggs, "Out with the Degree, In with the Badge," *InformEd*, August 13, 2013, http://www.opencolleges.edu.au/informed/features/badges-in-education/.

26. Duncan, "Digital Badges for Learning."

27. Briggs, "Out with the Degree," ¶ 30.

28. Kristi Oloffson, "A College Guarantees Job Offers—or Else a Refund," *Time*, April 7, 2010, http://content.time.com/time/nation/article/0,8599,1978286,00.html.

29. Margaret J. Wheatley, ed., *Leadership and the New Science: Discovering Order in a Chaotic World*, 3rd ed. (San Francisco: Berrett-Koehler Publishers, Inc., 2006), 76.

30. David K. Reynolds, *Playing Ball on Running Water: The Japanese Way to Building a Better Life* (New York: Quill, 1984), 1.

31. "Using Linked Data to Drive Education and Training Improvement," (Data Quality Campaign Research Brief, n.d.), http://files.eric.ed.gov.proxy .wm.edu/fulltext/ED539334.pdf.

32. "Leading the Way: Access. Success. Impact. 2013-2018," *West Virginia Higher Education Policy Commission*, accessed January 20, 2015, http://www .wvhepc.com/master-plan-leading-the-way/.

33. Janice Nahra Friedel, Zoë Mercedes Thornton, Mark M. D'Amico, and Stephen G. Katsinas, "Performance Based Funding: The National Landscape" (Tuscaloosa, AL: Education Policy Center, University of Alabama, 2013).

34. J. Stewart Black and Hal B. Gregerson, *It Starts with One: Changing Individuals Changes Organizations* (Upper Saddle River, NJ: Pearson Education, Inc., 2008).

35. Interview with James Lorenson.

36. Glenn DuBois, "Virginia 2013 and Beyond: Meeting the Workforce Imperative," (PowerPoint presentation, n.d.), accessed September 17, 2014, http://www.warner.senate.gov/public/_cache/files/9ed5f30f-c335-47d3-9ad6-1bcdcc5c274a/DuBois%20Prezi%20for%20Va%20Leadership%20Summit%20PDF%20File%2006.14.13.pdf.

37. "Rural Horseshoe Initiative," *Virginia's Community Colleges*, accessed September 17, 2014, http://www.vccs.edu/giving/rural-horseshoe-initiative/.

38. *The American College President 2012*.

39. Arthur Levine, "Educating School Leaders" (New York: The Educations School Project, 2005), http://www.edschools.org/pdf/final313.pdf.

40. "History of the Initiative," *The Carnegie Project on the Education Doctorate*, accessed December 14, 2014, http://cpedinitiative.org/about/history.

41. "Competencies for Community College Leaders," *American Association of Community Colleges*, accessed November 10, 2014, http://www.aacc.nche.edu/Resources/competencies/Pages/default.aspx.

42. *AACC Competencies for Community College Leaders* (Washington, DC: American Association for Community Colleges, 2014), 6, http://www.aacc.nche.edu/newsevents/Events/leadershipsuite/Documents/AACC_Core_Competencies_web.pdf.

43. *AACC Competencies for Community College Leaders*, 8.

44. *AACC Competencies for Community College Leaders*, 9.

45. *AACC Competencies for Community College Leaders*, 10.

46. *AACC Competencies for Community College Leaders*, 11.

47. *The American College President 2012*, 99.

48. Kotter, *Accelerate*.

49. Kotter, *Accelerate*, 7.

50. Pamela L. Eddy, *Community College Leadership: A Multidimensional Model for Leading Change* (Sterling, VA: Stylus Press, 2010).

51. Charles C. Kenney, *The Best Practice: How the New Quality Movement is Transforming Medicine* (New York: Public Affairs, 2008).

52. *The American College President 2012*.

53. U.S. Department of Education, National Center for Education Statistics, Integrated Postsecondary Education, "Table 264. Total fall enrollment in degree-granting institutions, by level and control of institution and race/ethnicity of student: Selected years, 1976 through 2011," http://nces.ed.gov/programs/digest/d12/tables/dt12_264.asp.

54. U.S. Department of Education, National Center for Education Statistics, Integrated Postsecondary Education, "Table 287. Employees in degree-granting institutions, by race/ethnicity, sex, employment status, control and

level of institution, and primary occupation: Fall 2011," http://nces.ed.gov/ programs/digest/d12/tables/dt12_287.asp.

55. Peter D. Eckel, Bryan J. Cook, and Jacqueline E. King (2009). *The CAO Census: A National Profile of Chief Academic Officers* (Washington, DC: The American Council on Education, 2009).

56. Susan R. Komives, Nance Lucas, and Timothy R. McMahon, *Exploring Leadership: For College Students Who Want to Make a Difference* (San Francisco: Jossey-Bass, 2013).

57. Pamela L. Eddy, "Developing Leaders: The Role of Competencies in Rural Community Colleges," *Community College Review* 41, no. 1 (2013): 20–43.

58. Carla A. Costello, "Women in the Academy: The Impact of Culture, Climate and Policies on Female Classified Staff," *NASPA Journal about Women in Higher Education* 5, no. 2 (2012): 99–114.

59. Regina L. Garza Mitchell and Pamela L. Eddy, "In the Middle: A Gendered View of Career Pathways of Mid-Level Community College Leaders," *Community College Journal of Research and Practice*, 32, no. 10 (2008): 793–811.

60. Marilyn J. Amey, *Breaking Tradition: New Community College Leadership Programs Meet 21st Century Needs* (Washington, DC: American Association of Community Colleges, 2006).

61. Kotter, *Accelerate*, 15.

62. Pamela L. Eddy and Michael Rao, "Leadership Development in Higher Education Programs," [Editor's Choice] *Community College Enterprise* 15, no. 2 (2009): 7–26.

63. Sydow and Alfred, *Re-visioning Community Colleges.*

64. Romano, Richard M., Barbara Townsend, and Ketevan Mamiseishvili. "Leaders in the Making: Profile and Perceptions of Students in Community College Doctoral Programs," *Community College Journal of Research and Practice* 33, no. 3–4 (2009): 309–320.

65. Barbara K Townsend and Sheila Bassoppo-Moyo, "The Ideal Community College Academic Affairs Administrator: An Inside View." (Paper presented at the Annual Conference of the Southern Association for Community College Research, Panama City, FL, August 5–7, 1996).

66. Frances Hesselbein and Eric K. Shinseki, *Be, Know, Do: Leadership the Army Way* (San Francisco: Jossey-Bass, 2004).

67. Kathleen McChesney and William Gavin, *Pick Up Your Own Brass: Leadership the FBI Way* (Dulles, VA: Potomac Books, 2011).

68. *The American College President 2012.*

69. Sean M Heuvel, "Culture Clash: A Case Study of the Issues that Non-Traditional College Presidents Face in Adjusting to Academic Culture" (PhD diss., College of William & Mary, 2014).

70. *The American College President 2012*.

71. Pamela L. Eddy, "Links between Leader Cognition, Power, and Change on Community College Campuses," *Journal of Applied Research in the Community College* 11, no. 2 (2004): 95–104.

5

STRATEGICALLY
LOOKING FORWARD

Effective leaders don't mobilize people and organizations because they see things in one way. . . . They can look at a complex organization's most difficult problems from many vantage points, which, together, give them a better appreciation for their options. And in responding to the challenges they face, they bring different mindsets to bear, and work in multiple modes.

—Ryan et al.[1]

The focus of this book is on thinking differently about leaders, leadership development, and what it means to lead colleges, specifically, community colleges, effectively into the future. Tried-and-true ways of the past will not suffice to meet the challenges and demands of an exponentially complex environment. Furthermore, leadership and management practices that work today may not be sufficient to position our colleges for the pursuit of opportunity in fast-paced markets that will be part of tomorrow's landscape.

Our colleges are no longer boundaried by geography or by policies and regulations or by systems and structure. Technology and the Internet have removed those borders—and with them, a rationale for stasis—by affording institutions connectivity around the world. We are boundaried by conventional ways of thinking and our own lack of imagination—literally by the limits of our mind. As such, community colleges will only be as good as the people working in them and the ability of leaders to tap tacit knowledge and skills throughout the organization. Borderless organizations require new approaches to leadership. Our focus in this chapter is on describing new leadership—why, who, and how.

Tomorrow's leaders are going to be leading colleges that bear little real resemblance to today's institutions. A few will be part of the Herculean task of organizational reinvention, and nearly all will be leading colleges that have been reinvented. In 2012, the *Chronicle of Higher Education* began to imagine this different higher-education landscape by taking "a variety of looks at some of the persistent conundrums of academe: how to staff the faculty and improve teaching . . . how to bring in more money, and how to help students and families pay for it all."[2]

The *Chronicle* invited readers to imagine starting a successful institution of higher education from scratch, and the ideas ranged from Costco University, a privatized model in which senior faculty would own the college and delegate basic administrative tasks to eliminate costly overhead and keeping tuition low, to a twenty-first-century monastic model where the college would "frighten away prospective students with strict vows of poverty, charity, and abstinence from social media."[3]

These start-from-scratch ideas, and countless others that are equally provocative and fun to entertain, point to the reality of the times. The model of higher education that has dominated the industry for centuries is broken, which means that all bets are off as the industry reshapes itself into a new model that suits its new clientele. It is this element of the unknown that makes the work of leadership today and into the future slightly intimidating and totally exhilarating.

We are getting glimpses into the future of higher education, including community colleges, through bold experiments and unproved models that have emerged at Western Governors University, Southern New Hampshire University, and in Australia's regional dual-sector (merged) institutions. Although the college of the future remains in bas-relief, there is no mystery about the key driver for whatever new model ultimately takes root. The higher education model of the future will be able to demonstrate a clear and compelling value proposition.

A NEW DAY

Leaders who have been in the business for a number of years may find their thought processes wired to demands and practices of the past, which can obscure vision of the future.[4] Contributing to this hardwiring problem is leadership development programming delivered in graduate programs and institutes, which is keyed to the development of operational skills and past constructs of what it means to be an effective leader.

These training programs filled a critical gap by developing a cadre of leaders for first-generation community colleges in the 1960s and 1970s. Yet, in the same way that community colleges today have reached a level of organizational maturity that has made them a traditional player in the higher education industry, so too have leadership development programs failed to evolve to address the capabilities required for leading community colleges tomorrow. Old tools and mental maps must now be discarded, and leaders must envision a different kind of future—one that requires them to ask hard questions, not only of themselves but also of their stakeholders and partners.

Leading a transformation—even when there is a clear mandate for transformation—requires attention to change and a willingness to tap into the talent and creativity of employees throughout the organization. When power is distributed, new sources of creativity are unleashed to mobilize change.[5] A new generation of organizational theorists has posited the importance of collaborative leadership[6] or connected leadership[7] for achieving transformative change, yet their ideas have not been widely embraced or converted into practice.

Ideally, "the work of leadership will be based on relationships rather than command and control models of the past and on networked processes and practices throughout the organization."[8] Building the relationships required to make networked leadership successful requires a shift in how stakeholder roles inside and outside the institution are conceived and deployed.

Substantive change in community colleges has been slow to unfold because the underlying architecture of institutions remains steadfastly locked to the past, and cultural norms and the hierarchy remain the same. As noted in chapter 4, Heimans and Timms[9] argue that "*new power* operates differently, like a current. It is created and exercised by many. It is open, participatory, and peer-driven. It uploads, and it distributes. Like water or electricity, it's most forceful when it surges. The objective with new power is to channel it, not hoard it." The energy of leaders distributed throughout the organization is channeled to achieve strategic priorities and to solve vexing problems. Although moving to a more sophisticated power model may not work for some colleges, combining this power model with a networked approach to leadership may be a means for colleges to initiate and sustain the innovation and creativity necessary to thrive in tomorrow's landscape.

When the power of top-down leaders converges with that of those leaders positioned throughout a network, energy is unleashed that moves in opposite directions unless channeled. Constructive energy has the potential to lead to lasting improvement, but as Kezar discovered in research on grassroots leadership, "Distributed leadership, perhaps wrongly, assumes shared interests between top-down and bottom-up leaders and our findings demonstrate and predict that grassroots leaders and those in positions of power often have differing interests."[10] Therefore, the creation of shared interest is a critical precursor to tapping into the leadership potential of individuals inside and outside the organization who are committed to the community college mission. Broad-based, networked leadership has significant potential for effecting change and transformation, but for successful implementation, the rules of the game must change.

NETWORKED LEADERSHIP

How can leaders embrace new rules and mobilize change? We can begin by moving beyond traditional conceptions of collaborative leadership toward distributed or networked leadership. As community colleges move from organizations that are loosely coupled with their communities to organizations that are tightly networked with partners in an expansive service region, so too must leaders make the transformation to a network. Rather than focusing exclusively on a college and its success, leaders must strategically partner with regional, national, and global business, not-for-profit, and educational organizations. The success of the network will become the success of the college—a uniquely different interpretation of institutional success than we find in colleges today.

Critical to building a networked organization is recasting the definition of a leader.[11] Helgeson's[12] seminal work on leadership conceived of a web of inclusion, which builds on individual relationships versus hierarchical position. For Helgeson, the organic nature of a web powers a connection among disparate parts, yet Helgeson's model of the web falls short of how we envision future leaders because it is based on the leader in the center and as the primary architect of the end product. It also focuses on individual relationships as opposed to organizational networks.

To understand networked leadership, we draw on social network analysis[13] to illustrate how leaders can create connections to navigate complex environments. Social networks encourage critical nodes or hubs in which connections are made both within an existing network and also between networks.

Intentionality is the basis of networked leadership. A happenstance network of individuals cannot leverage the complex connections required for innovation. It is not merely *who* is in the network but, *how* and *why* the connection is made that is important. Connections in networked leadership operate at both an individual and an institutional level. In Figure 5.1, individuals (distributed leaders) are represented by small circles. The larger circles represent the institutional connections among community colleges and business and educational and governmental organizations at the local, national, and international levels. Weak ties between organizations as represented by dashed lines actually provide a unique strength because they more readily bridge to different networks, thereby providing opportunity for value creation.

In chapter 4 we discussed the role of networks operating in tandem with the organizational hierarchy (represented here by the clear circles) and described how change can be mobilized through the enhanced focus on innovation and flexibility provided by a dual system.[14] It is the connection that exists between the innovative arm of the institution and the structures already in place that allow for change to become institutionalized and leveraged. Networked leaders serve as a critical component in this process because they link the institution to innovative business and education organizations that add value. Network partners

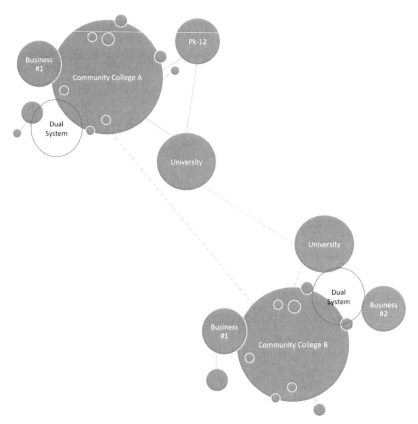

Figure 5.1. Networked Leadership

bring creative thinking and expertise to problem solving vastly beyond the resources of any one institution.

An example of networked leadership that appears to be working is the business model employed by Rio Salado College in the Maricopa Community College System. Rio Salado has long valued the collaborative nature of employee relationships, supporting instructors and staff working in teams and across silos and staying focused on the core mission of the college.

Rio adroitly establishes and carefully tends relationships with a network of organizations including universities, vendors, and employers. Rio established, for example, a fee-based partnership with Civitas Learning, which created a community of practice to improve the company's analytics product (driven by client input) and thereby advance mutually beneficial goals. Participating colleges in the network share their student demographics and performance data, and the company returns analytics that Rio and other colleges use to improve support services for their student population. Consequently, it is a win–win for Rio, Civitas Learning, and network colleges because together they are achieving results that improve student outcomes. The future for community colleges will be about high-performance networks that improve products, systems, and processes that drive student success.

Networked leadership is not simply the right thing to do for colleges experiencing resource constraints. It is also an important means for staving off competition and enhancing market share. Community colleges face formidable competition, and they are not as effective going it alone as they were previously. "New forms of education are springing up, with unconventional providers offering quality and convenience that cannot be duplicated by traditional providers."[15]

If leaders fail to get their arms around new forms of competition through information and insights provided by network partners, they will miss or overlook critical opportunities for growth and renewal. Networked leaders are actively engaged in real-time learning about where opportunities lie and how to strategically connect a college to those opportunities. Community college leaders in modern-day organizations, for example, are turning to divergent sources to gain business intelligence (e.g., borrowing from business and military experience to develop leaders).

The army's leadership manual provides valuable insights for leading in times of crisis when the stakes are particularly high. Pointedly, the army manual argues that "People need to do more than they are told; they need to participate actively and willingly"[16]—exactly the climate we believe networked leaders must work to create to set the stage for engaging talent throughout the college.

Networked leaders must not only understand the importance of distributing power throughout the organization, but they must also know how to digest and interpret information for decision making. In part, a problem with large-scale change is the plethora of information available to leaders, information in the form of simple prescriptions or step-by-step actions that provide *the* answer or quick fix. Ultimately, the networked leader must figure out what information is useful, what is not, and how to apply information to a particular context and set of circumstances.

Instead of seeing information as a valuable resource, leaders can become inured to the crush of information arriving in an already over-loaded inbox, and day-to-day demands leaving little time for research and thoughtful analysis. Networked leaders can navigate the onslaught of information and sift through it to find usable nuggets. They can also be proactive in seeking out information that is useful for problem solving.

WORKING WITH INFORMATION

The deluge of information coming at leaders is overwhelming. Each day, dozens of e-mail links for articles and executive reports, Twitter feeds, and podcasts come across a range of electronic devices for leaders to peruse. Add this to the vast amount of data that institutions collect and share in response to state and federal requirements, and it is easy to see that leaders are swimming, or more aptly drowning, in informa-tion. The trick is to sort, eliminate, make sense of, and effectively use information now at their fingertips in ways that help them to achieve important goals.

Resources

A number of information sources can be tapped and scanned for criti-cal information. If leaders restrict their focus to resources in education, they will overlook innovations in other fields and in different markets that have a critical bearing on community colleges. Researchers and scholars generate reams of text on factors contributing to student suc-cess or business processes that yield the biggest gains, yet much of this information remains beyond the eyes of leaders because researchers and practitioner circles rarely overlap.[17] At least two community col-lege research centers—the Office of Community College Research and Leadership (OCCRL) at the University of Illinois (http://occrl .illinois.edu/) and the Community College Research Center (CCRC) at Teacher's College (http://ccrc.tc.columbia.edu/)—have attempted to bridge this gap by providing a short synopsis of research and pushing this information out to end users via a simple listserv sign-up.

It is, however, also critical that leaders look beyond education resources. The business literature is replete with strategies for transforming organizations (e.g., *Harvard Business Review, The Economist,
Change Magazine, MIT Sloan Management Review,* etc.), and policy
think tanks providing executive summaries of research (e.g., The Institute of Higher Education Policy, Association of American Colleges and
Universities, American Association of Community Colleges, Association
of Community College Trustees) as do regional collaboratives (Midwest
Higher Education Compact, Southern Regional Education Board, New
England Board of Higher Education, Western Interstate Commission
for Higher Education). Tapping into expertise-for-hire is increasingly
easy given the ability to search on the Internet for needed skill sets.

Irrespective of the source, it is important to translate information
into the community college institutional context. It does little good to
borrow best practices from organizations that assume an infrastructure
incomparable to that of the community college. Intra- and interinstitu-
tional collaboration can help in sifting through information because it is
impossible for one person to read everything. A reading group or leaders' book club, such as that described previously in the book, is one simple, practical way to ensure that leaders access and process information
most relevant to the college. Group discussions can also be invaluable
in determining how individual leaders make sense of and apply information and their capacity for thinking and working together as a coalition.

Design Thinking

Busy leaders may think they do not have time to read, but networked
leaders must read broadly and deeply to gain a sense of what is hap-
pening both inside and outside higher education. Tracking larger social,
economic, and political forces helps to contextualize decisions and
anticipate future trends. Given the countless options, how does one
determine what information to access and how?

A simple answer is to be relentless in acquiring information about
key issues affecting the college and read those materials deeply to glean
information that can be useful to advance solutions. At the same time,
identify and regularly scan those few sources that intelligently track the

broader industry and related—or completely unrelated—industries to study and cross-fertilize divergent ideas. Do not rely exclusively on the written word.

Disciplined, direct interaction with reputable professionals inside and outside the organization and the industry is often the best way to acquire new ideas and information. The trick is to make careful choices about time invested, whom to interact with, and what to obtain through the interaction. This sounds, and is, common sensical, but far too many leaders fall into the trap of arrested development, prioritizing the weighty and time-consuming day-to-day tasks over their own ongoing growth. A leader's investment in self-development by maintaining industry and cross-industry currency should be a top priority.

Design thinking can help in this regard. It involves a "full spectrum of innovation activities with a human-centered ethos,"[18] and centers on internal staff who deliver service and customers on the receiving end of service. Here, change and innovation are guided by what people like or do not like about current practices and processes, and then figuring out how to give them exactly what they want.

Brown[19] outlined a design thinker's personality to include empathy (e.g., seeing the world from multiple perspectives), integrative thinking (e.g., connecting the dots across silos of information), optimism (e.g., no matter the challenges, believes there is a solution), experimentalism (e.g., questions assumptions of the way things are done to get to second-order change), and collaboration (e.g., works across organizational divides). Networked leaders must create the space necessary for design thinking to occur; it is a messy process that requires a systems perspective.

Cocreation

Community college leaders "need a common language to communicate effectively with internal and external stakeholders about innovation and the decisions that accompany it, which includes everything from resource allocation to program/service expectations."[20] The cocreation of programs and services with stakeholders helps to create a common language.

Throughout this book we have addressed how colleges partner in different ways with community organizations and agencies. These partnerships—more aptly called *networks*—should center on resource sharing and on defining and developing the skills needed for tomorrow's workforce. Companies with expanding capability to choose with whom they partner and how (e.g., through real or virtual connections) will look to the best provider for collaboration. They will also not be limited by geographical boundaries in seeking and finding partners.

It is entirely possible, in fact likely, that community colleges will be producing workers who live in the immediate geographic community but work for companies in other states, even other countries. To provide superior education and training, community colleges will need not only to be closely connected to industries and employers, but they will also need to cocreate programs, services, and delivery systems in partnership with them.

When we engage businesses and industries as cocreators of programs, how do we restructure college systems to support these collaborations?[21] Likewise, thinking of staff and faculty as coleaders and coproducers of strategic initiatives also requires adjusting organizational architecture and processes. Rio Salado College once again provides an example of how a college has transformed the way it does business through cocreation.

As Rufus Glasper, Chancellor of the Maricopa Community Colleges, explains, "Over time, Rio Salado College has intentionally built a business-oriented employee and management culture that meshes faculty and staff who are innovative thinkers, who embrace change, and who work collaboratively to remove barriers to higher education for students the college serves."[22] The collaborative culture of the institution builds on a systems approach, which exemplifies networked leadership. The unbundling of the faculty role has recast how the college views adjuncts and staff within an internal network.

Rio Salado is known for being a leader in online learning. The vast majority of its courses are taught online according to a block schedule that essentially allows students to enroll and commence a class any week within a given semester. Online learning has virtually unbundled the faculty role—"a process that occurs when tasks that were all normally performed by a single faculty member—such as course design, course development, presentation of content, interaction, assessment, evaluation, and advisement—are unbundled so that they can be performed by others or through distributed technologies."[23] These tasks may be performed by full-time faculty members, adjunct faculty, instructional designers, or other professionals, but the process requires collaboration on behalf of all involved.[24] Even though the transformation accomplished at Rio Salado may not transfer directly to other colleges, the process of change and disruption can be replicated.

Gerardo de los Santos, president and CEO of the League for Innovation, believes that community college leaders must make substantial changes to move our institutions forward.[25]

> We need to be thinking about the systemic, far-reaching changes or needs to be met that require a broad look at the institution or the organization, and be willing to take some risk with that. Now, the idea is educated risk, but risk nonetheless. [We should be] looking to guide these innovative next steps through the use of data and understanding how to use data properly to inform decision making. And we should be using quantitative and qualitative data to help guide the steps that we're taking. It's about enabling and cultivating a culture where you're allowing faculty, staff and leaders to take the risk and to be bold if it is in support of student success and completion and in support of our community.

This statement sums up the core ideas of networked leadership and the approach that must be taken by networked leaders. However, in this landscape of fast change, institutions need bedrock on which to forge strategy and priorities. Depending on institutional culture and leaders themselves, strategic change may be ignored, supported, or blocked, and the culture is based on shared values. Because values drive behavior, we close the book with a description of values that networked leaders would be wise to embrace as they lead transformation.

VALUES

Networked leadership, as presented in this book, centers on core values embraced by people throughout the organization. Core values and beliefs shape everything leaders do and, as a result, everything a college does. Accordingly, leaders must have an intimate understanding of core values, they must model them, and they must continually reinforce them in work and life.[26]

People

Community colleges are people-oriented organizations. Colleges do not produce goods and services; rather, they deliver education and promote learning in an attempt to help people achieve important goals. Similarly, instructors and staff are a critical resource in delivering service. They are a primary customer, if not the primary customer. Happy and motivated faculty and staff make for happy and motivated students. This changes the traditional customer equation and puts students *and* staff at the center of everything a college does.

Relationships

Networks are the core of the new leadership being described, but they are more than links that connect one organization to another or one person to another. Relationships are the basis for networks, and relationships are built on trust.[27] Using new forms of power, leaders must establish trust with partners inside and outside of organizational boundaries to successfully pursue the work of the organization.[28] Relationships are forged through distribution of power in contrast to centralization of authority.

Transparency

Social media have shifted how individuals think about privacy and information. Leaders experience greater success in advancing a change agenda through transparency and sharing of information. New generations of workers expect to actively shape and create many aspects of their lives, including work. Transparency is a must in an organizational context in which people want to participate on their own terms in contrast to simply doing what they are told.

Learning

Networked leaders value learning on multiple levels. Formal learning, as it occurs in educational settings, is obviously important. However, continuous personal and organizational learning is also essential. To move an institution forward, networked leaders must value and cultivate the learning that comes from intellectual pursuits, and the insights that are gained from trying new things, especially when there is potential for failure. Understanding *why* something failed and *how* to correct errors is part of an ongoing learning process in a turbulent environment.

Public Good

Community colleges are multimission, paradoxical organizations. Underlying the paradox and imbued through each mission component is the notion of the public good. We not only give back to the communities we live in, but we also help these communities and the people who live there to grow and flourish. Networked leaders recognize the importance of giving back and lifting up. They strive to bolster and sustain the health and well-being of the local community. Today the notion of public good is far-reaching. Public good extends beyond the immediate community to the nation and world. Networked leaders must be aware of the range of connections and possibilities in our flat world. Broadening our view of the public good ensures that community colleges will embrace values and ideals essential to good stewardship of communities, of the nation, of the world, and of the planet.

MOVING FORWARD

The surge of interest in leadership of several decades launched myriad concepts and theories about what it is that distinguishes individuals as effective leaders. Researchers in fields as varied as psychology, sociology, political science, and management all studied leaders and leadership, and even leaders themselves contemplated in countless books and articles what makes for effective leadership. In recent years, practitioners and theorists have converged on a central insight into leadership:

> Effective leaders don't mobilize people and organizations because they see things in one way; they succeed because they see things in many different ways. They can look at a complex organization's most difficult problems from many vantage points, which, together, give them a better appreciation for their options. And in responding to the challenges they face, they bring different mindsets to bear, and work in multiple modes.[29]

In these sundry modes, for example, leaders act as storytellers, politicians, coaches, enforcers, and culture builders. Leaders exercise their greatest power, however, by framing the issues at hand or, stated differently, deciding what the real problem is. Once the problems are framed, the options for solutions can be established. "More broadly, leaders influence their organizations by deciding what the organization should pay attention to and then providing ways of looking at it."[30] In this book, we argue that this type of generative thinking, the processes that leaders and groups use to frame problems and make sense of ambiguous situations, can be converted into systematic practices. At its core, network leaders position themselves as active learners at the organization's boundaries because that is where they are most likely to figure out the real problems to be solved.

The challenges facing community colleges require not only a different type of thinking than in the past. Leaders who effectively build and use networks to fulfill the community college mission will be poised to gain the most from talent inside and outside the organization. The Markle Economic Future Initiative argues that "America is in the early phase of a profound transition in its economy and society—on the frontier of changes that will touch the rest of the world."[31] We concur.

In this fast-paced, topsy-turvy environment, community colleges will require networked leadership to successfully transform into the robust education providers that our country will depend on to meet to societal demands. The ideas presented in this book will provide current and aspiring leaders with resources to lead the way, as well as benchmarks for developing tomorrow's leaders. Our colleges and their students expect and should receive nothing less.

NOTES

1. William Ryan, Richard Chait, and Barbara Taylor, "Governance as Leadership: Bringing New Governing Mindsets to Old Challenges," Board Source, 2008, http://www.michaeldavidson.biz/downloads/Leadership.pdf.

2. Scott Carlson, "College Reinvented," *Chronicle of Higher Education* (October 15, 2012).

3. Carlson, "College Reinvented."

4. Black and Gregerson, *Leading Strategic Change*.

5. Jeremy Heimans and Henry Timms, "Understanding 'New Power,'" *Harvard Business Review* 92, no. 12 (2014): 48–56.

6. Gil Hickman, *Leading Change in Multiple Contexts: Concepts and Practices in Organizational Community, Political, Social, and Global Change Settings* (Thousand Oaks, CA: Sage, 2010).

7. Jean Lipman-Blumen, *Connective Leadership: Managing in a Changing World* (San Francisco: Jossey-Bass, 1996)

8. Kay Hempsall, "Developing Leadership in Higher Education: Perspectives from the USA, the UK and Australia," *Journal of Higher Education Policy and Management* 36, no. 4 (2014): 383.

9. Heimans and Timms, "Understanding 'New Power,'" ¶ 5.

10. Adrianna Kezar, "Bottom-Up/Top-Down Leadership: Contradiction or Hidden Phenomenon," *Journal of Higher Education* 83, no. 5 (2012): 753.

11. Joan Williams, *Unbending Gender: Why Family and Work Conflict and What to Do about It* (New York: Oxford University Press, 2000).

12. Sally Helgeson, *The Web of Inclusion: A New Architecture for Building Great Organizations* (New York: Currency/Doubleday, 1995).

13. Peter J. Carrington, John Scott, and Stanley Wasserman, *Models and Methods in Social Network Analysis* (New York: Cambridge University Press, 2005).

14. Kotter, *Accelerate*.

15. The Markle Economic Future Initiative, *Rework America*, 11.

16. Frances Hesselbein and Eric K. Shinseki, *Be, Know, Do: Leadership the Army Way* (San Francisco: Jossey-Bass, 2004), 5.

17. Barbara K Townsend, Debra Bragg, and Mary Kinnick, "Who Writes the Most About Community Colleges? An Analysis of Selected Academic and Practitioner-Oriented Journals," *Community College Journal of Research and Practice* 27, no. 1 (January 2003): 41–49.

18. Tim Brown, "Design Thinking," *Harvard Business Review* 86, no. 6 (2008): 86.

19. Brown, "Design Thinking," 87.

20. Mario Martinez, "A Conceptual Foundation for Understanding Innovation in American Community Colleges," in *Disruptive Innovation in Community College*, ed. Rufus Glasper and Gerardo E. de los Santos (Chandler, AZ: League for Innovation in the Community College, 2013), 10.

21. Steven Mintz, "Students as Producers, Students as Partners," *Inside Higher Ed* (blog), December 10, 2014, https://www.insidehighered.com/blogs/higher-ed-beta/students-producers-students-partners.

22. Rufus Glasper, "The Disruptive Revolution in Academe: Community Colleges as Disruptive Innovators," in *Disruptive Innovation in Community*

College, ed. Rufus Glasper and Gerardo E. de los Santos (Chandler, AZ: League for Innovation in the Community College, 2013), 28.

23. Vernon C. Smith, "The Unbundling and Rebundling of the Faculty Role in E-Learning Community College Courses" (PhD diss., The University of Arizona, 2008), 13.

24. Vernon C. Smith and Gary Rhoades, "Community College Faculty and Web-Based Classes," *Thought and Action* 22 (2006): 97–110.

25. Interview with Gerardo de los Santos, president and CEO of the League for Innovation in the Community College, Chandler, Arizona, October 22, 2013.

26. Hesselbein and Shinseki, *Be, Know, Do.*

27. Megan Tschannen-Moran and Wayne K. Hoy, "A Multidisciplinary Analysis of the Nature, Meaning, and Measurement of Trust," *Review of Educational Research*, 70, no. 4 (2000): 547–593.

28. Herminia Ibarra and Mark Lee Hunter, "How Leaders Create and Use Networks," *Harvard Business Review* (2007).

29. Ryan et al., "Governance as Leadership."

30. Ryan et al., "Governance as Leadership."

31. The Markle Economic Future Initiative, *Rework America*, 5.

INDEX

ABOUT THE AUTHORS

Pamela L. Eddy is a professor in Educational Policy, Planning and Leadership at the College of William and Mary. Her research interests include community college leadership and development, gender roles in higher education, and faculty development. Eddy is the author or coauthor of numerous books on leadership.

Debbie Sydow is president of Richard Bland College, an affiliate of the College of William and Mary in Virginia. She is President Emerita and Distinguished Professor of English at the State University of New York's (SUNY) Onondaga Community College and coeditor of the Futures Series on Community Colleges.

Richard Alfred is Emeritus Professor of Higher Education at the University of Michigan. He is coeditor of the Futures Series on Community Colleges and Founding Director of the Center for Community College Development. Alfred has published widely in the fields of management and leadership, organizational change and development, and effectiveness and has consulted extensively with colleges engaged in transformation.

Regina Garza Mitchell is assistant professor of Higher Education Leadership in the Department of Educational Leadership, Research, and Technology at Western Michigan University. Previously she served as a senior administrator at Texas State Technical College–Harlingen.